Weight Training Everyone

Third Edition

Rich Tuten

Clancy Moore

Virgil Knight

Hunter Textbooks Inc.

Special Acknowledgments:

Cover photo: Copyright 1989 by Tyler Cox. All rights reserved.
Models for cover: Jodie Bowman and William Evans

Models for photographs provided for Third Edition:
Trent Knight, Jason Gigot, Megan Murphy

Copyright 1990 by Hunter Textbooks, Inc.

ISBN 0-99725-139-0

All rights reserved. No part of this publication may be reproduced in any form whatsoever without prior permission of the publisher.

Inquiries should be addressed to:

 Hunter Textbooks Inc.

823 Reynolda Road
Winston-Salem, North Carolina 27104

Preface

In the past few years, a phenomenal increase has occurred in the popularity of weight training—first as a rehabilitation technique for World War II servicemen (bringing about a gradual acceptance by the medical profession), then as a training technique for athletes. Presently, the public is showing a tremendous interest in the sport of "pumping iron."

It is because of this newly awakened interest that the authors of *Weight Training—Everyone* decided to make available to the general public the experience and knowledge which they have acquired in developing strength for male and female athletes at three major universities and a noted National League Football team.

Acknowledgments

The authors of this book gratefully acknowledge the many suggestions and insights rendered by their colleagues.

Clancy Moore
Rich Tuten
Virgil Knight

CONTENTS

1	Weight Training — Today and Yesterday	1
2	Equipment	10
3	Questions Most Often Asked	21
4	Scientific Principles	45
5	Stretching and Avoiding Injury	51
6	Basic Fundamentals	73
7	Establishing Your Program	80
8	Free Weight Lifts	85
9	The Universal Machine	113
10	The Nautilus Concept	121
11	Special Weight Training Programs	153

Appendixes: A, References, 209; B, Muscles of the Body, 210; C, Kilo/Pound Conversion Chart, 212; D, Chapter Evaluations, 213; E, Weight Training Examination, 233; F, Blank Charts, 237

A foreword on physical conditioning

Being in good physical condition or "being in shape" is a combination of many things, and since strength is one of the most important parts, improving strength and developing the body is the purpose of our text. However, we cannot emphasize too strongly the importance of including a sound cardiovascular program, such as Dr. Kenneth Cooper's aerobics, as a part of your total fitness program.

Another very important part of physical conditioning and weight training is sound dietary practices such as recommended by Jean Mayer, the noted Harvard expert on nutrition. Dr. Mayer's book, *Overweight,* is an excellent text in a field noted for its quackery and chicanery.

One word of caution: if you are an adult and have not been exercising on a regular basis, you should first see your doctor as a precautionary measure. Then begin your program; but by all means, whether young or old, **go slowly!**

Chapter 1

WEIGHT TRAINING — TODAY AND YESTERDAY

Yesterday and Today

WHY WEIGHT TRAINING?

The odds are that you are presently asking yourself why you chose an activity involving so much "hard work." Actually, there are a number of good reasons why weight training appeals to so many men and women and why it is rapidly becoming one of the most popular of sports. Researchers agree that many people are dissatisfied with the shape of their bodies, and, while weight training can only do so much, it has been proven that certain exercises can be chosen which will develop selected muscles and specific parts of the body.

If you are the type of person who discourages easily and must see observable gains, then weight training should be your cup of tea. The serious weight trainer can often measure some gains after only a few short weeks. Since it is customary to keep close records of the amount of weight lifted for each exercise, you will be able to see exactly how much progress you are making in developing your strength.

Also, if you consider yourself less than highly coordinated and seem to be less able to compete in those things requiring hand-eye coordination, weight training should be for you, as the exercises and lifts involve simple skills and are very easy to learn.

Another appealing feature of the sport is the small amount of equipment needed. Of course, some of the machines pictured in this book are very expensive; however, a simple set of weights and bar will allow you to engage in an excellent program at a very modest cost.

Are you easily bored? Weight training offers limitless variations which can be used to avoid the "blahs." Another nice feature is that you don't have to have a team or a foursome to participate. Of course, some lifts can be dangerous, and when these are performed, assistance is a must.

Want to improve your ability in a sport at which you already feel reasonably competent? Most serious athletes engage in some form of weight training and there is substantial evidence that this activity improves performance in almost all sports.

ORIGIN OF WEIGHT TRAINING

Man's first strength contest was not recorded; however, the wager was probably substantial — either killing or being killed by some prehistoric animal. The advent of civilization found man growing more adept at subjugating most of the world's wild animals with one exception — his own kind, with which he has continued to fight, whether over territory, food, wealth, the opposite sex, or his own foolish pride.

With the arrival of recorded history we find scenes of wrestlers and other strong men being sculptured and painted by the Egyptians and Greeks. Possibly the most famous of these early lifters was Milo of Crotona. This incredible athlete was one of the first to practice progressive weight training. He did so by lifting a calf several times a week. Of course as the calf grew and added weight, Milo also adjusted by building his muscle strength until eventually he was the only human strong enough to handle the fully grown beast.

It is said that Milo's pride and strength ultimately caused his death. The story goes that the strong man was going through a deep forest and noticed a wedge deeply imbedded in a tree stump. Accepting the stump as a challenge, he attempted to tear it apart with his bare hands. However, as the wedge fell out, his hand or hands became caught in the vacated crack and he was unable to free himself. The tale has it that the animals of the forest eventually devoured him at the scene of his entrapment.

The earliest recorded weight training objects were dumbbell-like devices developed by the Greeks and called halteres. The Irish had their own method which consisted of lifting huge boulders. Perhaps this is why Julius Caesar is reputed to have once said, "Forget Ireland; the Irish are wild men and will never make good slaves."

The term dumbbell is believed to have originated in England in the 1600s. The original versions were constructed by mounting regular bells, without clappers, on each end of an axe handle or stick — hence the term "dumb bell."

About 1728, John Paugh, another early weight trainer, decided that apparatus involving dumbbells would be a valuable training aid. This concept was later adapted by Frederick Jahn, who founded the German gymnastics and strength movement.

This organization was later transplanted in America in the 1800s by migrating Germans and became known as the Turner Society, serving as a forerunner to the YMCA movement.

During the later 1800s, George Hackensmidt of Germany, who bent coins with his fingers, and other strong men like Eugene Sandow and Arthur Saxon performed in circuses and on stage. Unfortunately, many of these old time strength merchants did not present a desirable public image due to their being extremely fat. Because of this and the environment usually associated with weight lifting, the public indicated little interest in the sport during this era.

Undoubtedly the first Olympic games in 1896 and the succeeding games contributed greatly to the rising popularity of weight lifting and weight training. Until World War II weight training continued to attract only a few professional strong men and a small group of competetive weight lifters. Athletic coaches generally admonished their athletes to avoid weight training for fear of becoming "muscle bound."

The man most responsible for correcting these misconceptions was an American army doctor named T.L. DeLorme. Dr. DeLorme, working with soldiers requiring physical rehabilitation, introduced equipment and techniques which rapidly caused an about-face by the medical profession. This in turn led to acceptance by coaches and physical educators.

WEIGHT TRAINING TODAY

Today's weight trainers are generally classified into five categories. However, a sixth group is rapidly emerging, and it is this group which precipitated the writing of this text.

Power Lifters — These people are primarily interested in developing raw strength and generally compete in only three power lifts — the squat, bench press, and dead lift. If some other form of lift is added, the meet is usually called an Odd Lifts Meet. In training, power lifters use extremely heavy weights, many sets, and few repetitions.

Weight Lifters — Weight lifters are competitive performers with a primary interest in developing the techniques necessary for the two lifts used in Olympic competition, the two-hand snatch and the two-hand clean and jerk. They usually work at close to maximum lifting and rarely do more than three repetitions of any exercise at a given time.

Athletes — Almost all high-powered athletic programs now prescribe weight training as a method of training for competition, particularly in the pre-season and post-season periods.

The key principle underlying the selection of weight training exercises for any athletic activity is that the athlete should do those exercises which duplicate the muscle and joint movements used in performing the sport and in developing general all-around strength.

This principle, coupled with regular workouts and practice in the sport, will result in increased strength and power with no measurable loss of precision or skill. Many athletes and coaches, however, prefer to do their heavy weight training in the "off season." Also, most prefer to end all weight training exercise from two to four days prior to competition.

Patients — There are two basic reasons why doctors prescribe progressive resistance (weight training) exercise for a patient. The most important, from a medical standpoint, is the restoration of strength; however, a patient may be more concerned with his or her appearance rather than ability to function at 100%. Fortunately the two often go hand in hand so that both objectives can be attained at the same time.

Body Builders — These people are most interested in developing physique through massive musculature and great definition. They are not so much interested in strength and generally are not outstanding athletes. They usually achieve their goals by doing repeated sets of an exercise with a high number of repetitions in each set. This tends to define the muscles by engorging the muscle tissue with blood.

Jane and John Doe (average students) — Many women and men fit none of the above classifications and belong to the sixth category for which this text is written. Most participate in some type of sport and are mildly interested in improving their performance. Some have a weight problem and would like to firm up a little, take a little off, and/or put a little on, here and there. Some would like to be a little stronger but do not care to become heavily muscled. A few may have an old or new injury which they would like to strengthen. Or it may be that television and other forms of the media have whetted their interest with pictures of men and women "pumping iron."

Whatever your reason for engaging in weight training, we hope the following pages will provide you with what you are seeking. There is one admonition. **YOU WILL ONLY GET OUT OF WEIGHT TRAINING WHAT YOU PUT INTO IT.** So good luck with your program!

Weight Training is for EVERYONE!!

A WEIGHT TRAINING VOCABULARY

ABDUCTION — Moving outward or away from the body's center line.

ADDUCTION — Moving inward or toward the body's center line.

ANABOLIC STEROIDS — Synthetic hormones used to stimulate growth of protein tissue.

BAR — The bar is steel, approximates one inch in diameter, and ranges from one to seven feet in length. The most common bars are five and six feet. The weight of a five- to six-foot bar will approximate twenty-five to thirty pounds.

BENCH PRESS — This is probably the one best exercise for the upper body. The exerciser takes a supine position on a bench and moves a weight from chest level to a straight arm position.

CLEAN AND JERK — An Olympic movement requiring the weight to be carried to the chest in one move and then thrust over one's head in a second movement.

COLLARS — These are metal devices which slip over the bar (usually two outside and two inside) and lock the weight plates in place.

CUTS — A form of muscular definition reflected by separations between groups of muscle fibers.

DEAD LIFT — An exercise used to develop back strength and grip strength. The lifter usually uses a regular and a reverse grip, crouches with head up and back down, then moves smoothly to an erect standing position with the bar resting across the upper thighs.

DUMBBELL — The dumbbells look like short barbells from eight to twenty inches long. They are usually cast in one piece, are a fixed poundage, and have round or hexagonal ends.

ELASTIC REBOUND — Muscle flexion that is immediately followed by extension. This reduces the loss of heat in the muscle and the stored elastic energy.

EXTENSION — The unfolding or extension of two body parts. A pressing movement would be the best example.

FLEXION — This occurs when two body parts that are connected at a joint are brought closer together. A curl is the best example.

HEAD STRAP — A belt-like piece of canvas webbing that is worn around the top of one's head. There is a chain attached to the strap and weights are then fastened to the chain. This device is primarily used to develop the neck muscles.

HYPERTROPHY — The enlarging of muscle tissue.

INCLINE-DECLINE BOARDS — These are padded boards that are positioned in either an upward or downward slope. Their use allows the various muscle groups to be exercised at different angles and body positions.

IRON BOOTS — These are shoe-like devices which attach to the feet for the purpose of strengthening leg and hip movements. Plates may be attached to the boots to increase resistance. A more recent innovation is a boot which allows a person to hook on to a chinning bar and to hang head down.

ISOKINETIC — A form of exercise in which muscle tension is kept at a maximum through the full range of muscle movement.

ISOMETRIC — The static contraction of a muscle group in which the joint angle and the muscle length remain constant.

ISOTONIC — A concentric muscle contraction which shortens the muscle and moves a load.

LAT MACHINE — This machine provides a downward resistance from an overhead position. Its primary use is to develop a broad upper back and stronger latissimus dorsi muscles.

LOAD — The actual amount of weight lifted in completing a weight training exercise movement.

MUSCULAR ENDURANCE — The ability of the muscles to continue to contract or do work over a long period of time.

NEGATIVE EXERCISE — Exercise that limits movements by eccentric contractions while increasing the muscle's length. Example: lowering a weight under complete control.

NEGATIVE EMPHASIZED EXERCISE — Exercise in which additional resistance is placed on the body during a negative movement but is removed during the positive phase. Example: placing a weight plate on the chest during the downward movement of a sit-up.

NEGATIVE ACCENTUATED EXERCISE — Exercise in which the resistance (weights) is lifted with two limbs and slowly lowered with one.

NEGATIVE ONLY EXERCISE — Exercise in which the positive part of a lift or exercise is done by another person or persons on the trainee's legs. The heavier than normal weight is then lowered by the lifter.

OLYMPIC LIFTING — This involves two lifts, the snatch and the clean and jerk.

OVERLOADING — When you are able to do the desired number of repetitions during the first set you should increase the poundage or resistance by approximately 5%. The most frequent weight increase is 5 pounds.

POWER — The combination of strength and speed on the application of strength to an "explosive" movement.

POWER CLEAN — Lift in which the weight is moved from knee level to the shoulders in one movement.

POWER LIFTING — A type of weight lifting competition which requires participants to lift the greatest amount of weight in three events: the bench press, the squat, and the dead lift. This is probably more of a test of sheer strength than of explosive power.

PRONE — A face downward position.

REPS — Repetitions — A weight training repetition occurs whenever a complete cycle of movements is finished. Repetitions are frequently designated as a capital R.

SNATCH — A single continuous movement that pulls the barbell from the floor to an overhead position with the arms fully straightened. The lifter may squat or split to assist in getting under the weight, but then must straighten, holding the barbell under control.

SQUAT — A lift in which the barbell is placed across the neck and back of the lifter's shoulders. The lifter sinks in a controlled crouch until the seat is approximately parallel to the floor and then straightens to an upright standing position.

STANDARDS — Metal devices which support barbells, when not in use, at a desired height off the floor.

STICKING POINT — A lifting point at which the greatest effort is called upon to complete the move. This happens when the joint angle is least efficient in terms of mechanical efficiency.

SUPINE — A horizontal position with the weight trainer lying on the back.

TEN EXECUTIONS MAX — This is the maximum number of repetitions of an exercise that can be done with a set poundage. The person is unable to do more than 10 Reps at this poundage.

BIBLIOGRAPHY

AAHPER, *Weight Training in Sports and Physical Education,* Washington, D.C.

Murray, Jim, *Contemporary Weight Training,* Contemporary Books, Inc., Chicago, Ill.

Rasch, Philip, *Weight Training,* William C. Brown, Dubuque, Iowa.

See Chapter Evaluation , Appendix D.

Chapter 2

EQUIPMENT

One of the purposes of this book is to provide a series of weight training exercises which can either be practiced in your home or in the gym. Of course, a minimum amount of equipment is required for any activity, but, unlike many sports, there are no recurring costs in weight training once you have access to a basic set of weights.

Since you probably are not yet an Olympic caliber lifter, you do not have to worry about having the most expensive bar and weights. What you will need can be acquired for less than $50-$100 and should include the following:

1. A long bar, but lighter than the Olympic bar
2. Two short bars
3. A selection of plastic-covered weights that will fit interchangeably on your bar.

Plastic-covered weights are recommended because they allow you to practice more quietly and are much easier on your floors. Most beginning weight sets average about 110-120 pounds and, if you can buy additional plates as your strength increases, should prove more than adequate. If you have a choice as to $2^1/_2$-pound plates versus 5-pound plates, we recommend the smaller plates since you will be able to add weight more gradually. You probably haven't thought about it, but if you only have 5-pound weights and must add two to balance the bar, then you are dealing with a 10-pound increment, and this gets mighty heavy on some lifts.

NONADJUSTABLE WEIGHTS

Most gymnasiums have many nonadjustable weights. However, unless you can afford a different set of dumbbells for each weight level, we recommend interchangeable weights. Since weight training is based on **progressive resistance,** it will be necessary that you have flexibility in increasing your weights as you develop additional strength.

Dumbbells offer the advantage of forcing a person to do an equal amount of work with each arm. This prevents you from unconsciously shifting part of the load to your stronger or better coordinated arm. Another advantage is that the hands can be rotated as the weight is lifted or curled, thus increasing the contraction of a muscle or group of muscles.

Figure 2-1 includes a typical rack of fixed weights (dumbbells), a straight barbell and rack, a barbell on protective floor covering, and several inclined benches.

Figure 2-1. Some of the equipment used in weight training

Figure 2-2. The incline bench

The Incline Bench — The incline bench (See Fig. 2-2) is a very useful device for pressing with a barbell or dumbbells or for curling with dumbbells. The primary value of the incline is that it permits you to press straight up, while working the deltoids and the pectorals, at about the same angle of release for the shot or discus.

Short Barbell — Can be used for curls, sitting military, wrist work, toe raises, high pulls, shrugs, straight leg dead lift, light weight squats, and many other exercises.

Figure 2-3. Short barbell

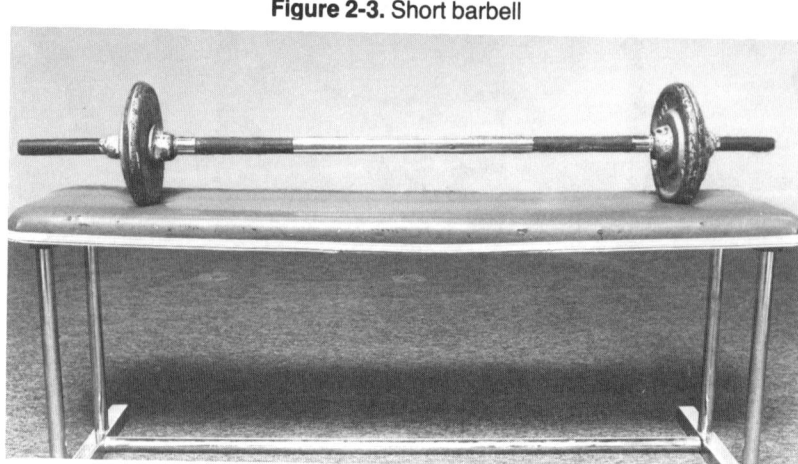

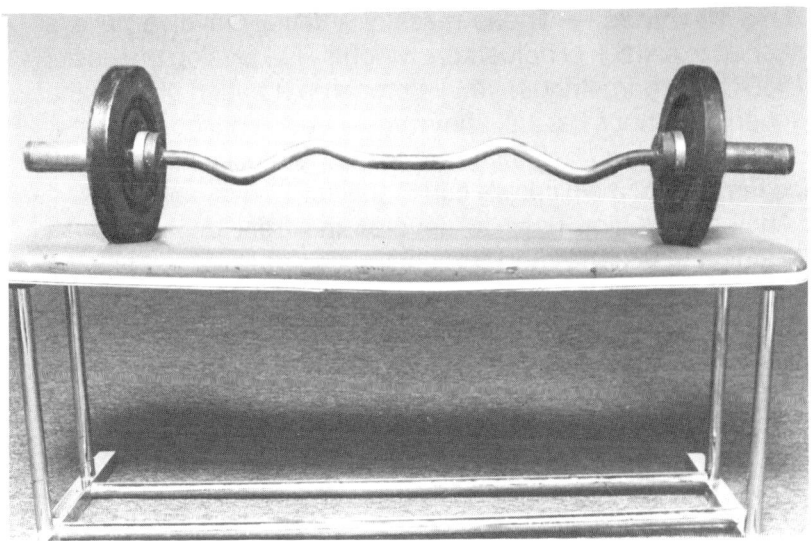

Figure 2-4. The E-Z curl bar

The E-Z curl bar can be used for biceps/curls, forearm curl or French curl, triceps extension, triceps press, close grip bench press, high pulls, and other exercises.

The squat rack is mainly used for squat lifts. It also is used for the military press and toe raises.

Figure 2-5. The squat rack

Leg Machines — These machines usually involve pulleys attached to a stack of adjustable weights. To develop the backs of your legs (hamstrings) you lie prone on a bench placing the padded resistance bar just above your heels. You then flex your legs to bring your heels as close to your buttocks as possible. See Fig. 2-6 for a typical leg curl machine.

Another variation used to develop the front thigh muscles (quadriceps) is performed by either sitting or lying and placing your instep against the resistance bar and lifting upward. See Fig. 2-7.

Leg press machines utilize most of the muscles of the lower back, buttocks, and upper legs. See Figs. 2-8, 2-9 and 2-10.

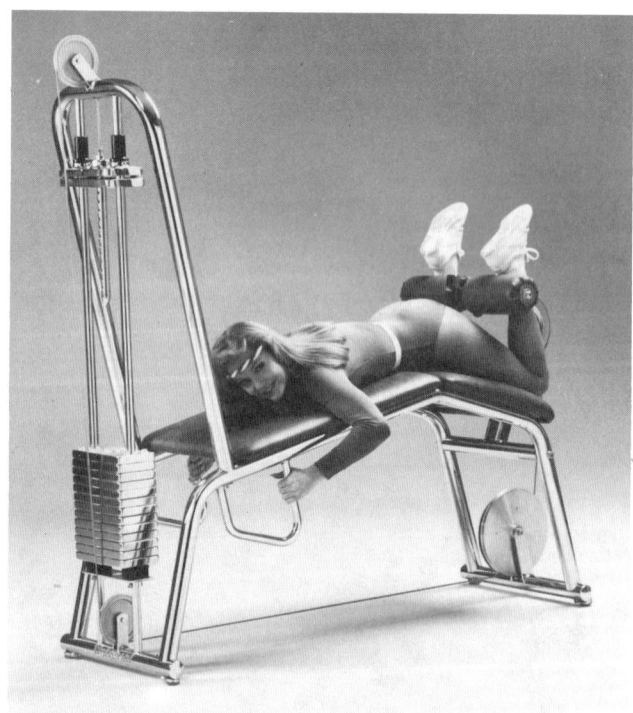

Figure 2-6. Universal leg curl machine.

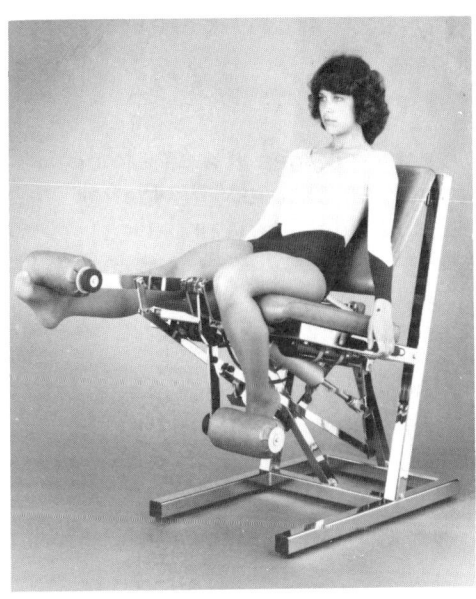

Figure 2-8. The A.M.F. leg press machine is found in many gyms and is excellent for heavy leg work.

Figure 2-7. Keiser leg extension machine.

Figure 2-9. Cybex leg press machine.

Figure 2-10. Nautilus leg press machine.

The "Lat Machine" — This machine comes in a variety of forms (See Figs. 2-11, 2-12) and is an excellent device for developing the latissimus dorsi muscles that give your back a V shape. While chinning with a wide grip will do the same thing, "Lat Machines" offer the advantage of beginning with a weight less than your full body weight and gradually working up.

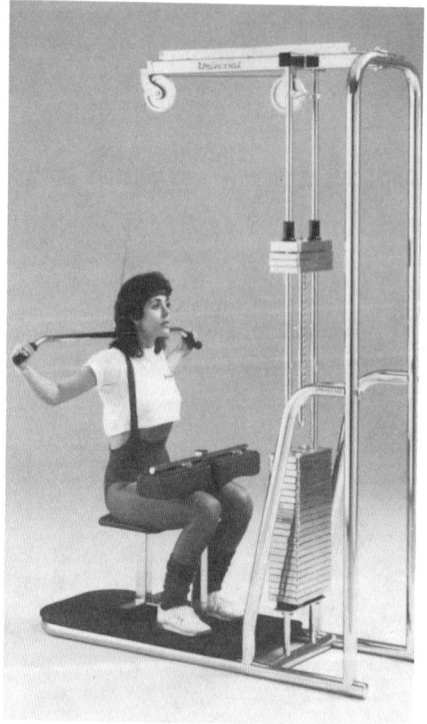

Figure 2-11. Universal pull down machine.

Figure 2-12. Nautilus torso arm machine.

Arm, Chest, and Shoulder Machine — These machines come in a variety of shapes and sizes. Basically all function by providing variable resistance to the muscles of the upper torso. See Figs. 2-13 and 2-14 for examples.

Figure 2-13. Cybex Eagle Fly machine.

Figure 2-14. Universal double triceps machine.

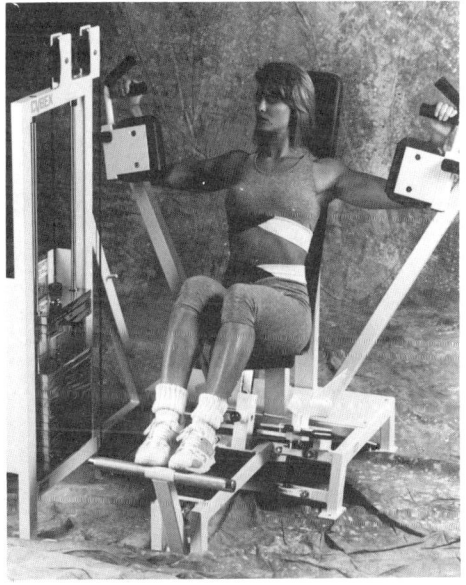

The Schwinn Bowflex is a relatively new concept that we think will gain acceptance. The concept is based on the use of flexible "power rods" that provide linear progressive resistance. The Bowflex machine comes with rods that are calibrated in pounds from 5-210. Additional resistance to over 400 pounds is available. The rods appear to work the muscles through their entire range of motion. And, unlike free weights, the lifter never loses resistance during an exercise. Additional features include:

* Bowflex can be folded up and rolled away for compact storage. It weighs only 72 pounds.
* It is practically silent because the resistance is in the bowing rods.
* Quick change overs—all that is necessary is to hook into additional rods.
* Because of the bilateral design strong muscles can not compensate for weak ones. Thus it helps produce better body symmetry.

Figures 2-15 and 2-16. The Schwinn Bowflex

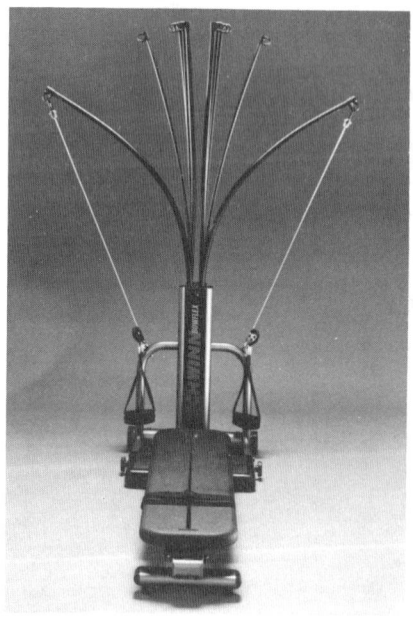
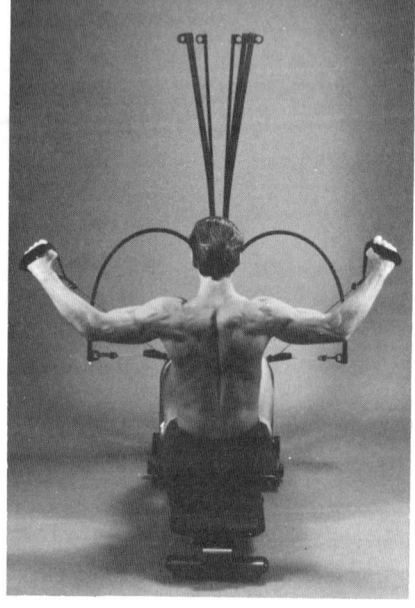

The Box Jump — Great for explosion, flexibility, speed, quickness, and vertical jump. Box dimensions — 42 × 42 × 42 padded with rubber. Procedure — standing 18 inches from box jump from a squatted position, landing with both feet on rubber padded top.

Figure 2-17 *(top)* and **Figure 2-18** *(bottom).* The box jump.

See Chapter Evaluation , Appendix D.

Chapter 3
QUESTIONS MOST OFTEN ASKED

How important is physical fitness to "good health"? While good health and physical fitness are related it must be noted that regular physical activity produces some health benefits that are not necessarily directly related to a high degree of physical fitness. For instance, research studies among adults have shown that exercise on a regular basis is directly related to reduced cases of mental health problems (depression), diabetes, osteoporosis, and certain types of cancer.

That regular low intensity exercise can provide some protection has been further documented by Paffenbarger and others, in their Harvard alumni study, and by Laporte's group of researchers.

Will I be "physically fit" if I weight train? Although weight training is the best way to develop strength, this does not mean you will be physically fit. Most research indicates little improvement in cardiorespiratory capacity, unless an aerobic program is utilized in a prescriptive manner.

Is there a point in life when it is too late to begin an exercise program? It is now recognized that many problems long attributed to aging are, in fact, infirmities that could be avoided if people would only be more active.

The list of infirmities includes reduced muscle strength, shortness of breath, slowed reflexes, soft bones, stiffness, senility, and a

It's never too late!

double chin. We now know these "symptoms of aging" can be limited by one of the most natural activities — walking. Exercise makes us breathe and thus increase the oxygenation process at the molecular level. After age 20, we process an average of one percent less oxygen every year. The result of this cutback is a commensurate decline in cellular activity. In reality, our bodies begin to suffocate. Studies have shown that people who remain active as they get older can maintain breathing capacities equal to people 40 years their junior.

The human body responds to physical stress by adapting and growing stronger. Heart and lungs don't get tired as we get older, they get lazy. Bones respond to environmental stress (exercise) accordingly. As bones are stressed by muscular contraction and compressional impacts of exercise, they respond by taking on more calcium and phosphorus — getting thicker, denser, and stronger as a result. The skin becomes thicker, stronger, and more elastic as a result of good oxygen uptake capacity. Skin reflects adaptation of habitual endurance training by increasing its mass and strengthening its structure.

Exercise seems to strengthen nerve tissue in about the same manner as it does muscles. The increased enzyme activity and abundant blood flow caused by exercise appear to safeguard the overall health of the central nervous system — brain included.

What are the latest statistics on low back pain and its causes? First of all, low back pain remains a major problem. With about 70 million problem cases and nearly seven million new cases yearly, many people are becoming dependent upon medication for pain. Injuries and a number of other disorders continue to trigger this condition. However, researchers have determined that most low back pain problems resulted from muscle tension, muscle weakness, and muscle spasms. A strong argument for selected weight training exercises.

Can weight training prevent osteoporosis (loss of bone mass)? Considerable losses of bone mass have been experienced by American and Soviet astronauts who have remained in space for 84 days or more. When bone does not experience normal stress, whether due to lack of gravity or lack of activity, as in the elderly, it will begin to deteriorate. Research as reported by Whaler, Steel, and Carter at Stanford University indicates that "for bone mass maintenance, it is much more important to have activities with high loads and high stresses than activities with lots of cycles." If they are correct, then weight training should build bone mass better than swimming or jogging. Of course, proper blood calcium levels are necessary, plus, in some cases, estrogen for some women who have reached menopause.

What is the best age for young people to begin strength training? Most doctors advise ages 14-16. However, as we know, our athletic programs begin earlier than that. Many coaches and trainers believe that strength training should begin at the ages of 8-9-10, but in the form of games rather than formal weight training.

Is weight training expensive? Only if you belong to a swanky spa or fitness club. Actually, weight training is one of the cheapest forms of exercise. A good barbell set will cost from $50 to $100 and will never wear out. You can't say that about a bicycle, tennis racket, or a set of golf clubs.

Is it true there has been a drop in the number of exercisers in the last few years? Dr. Kenneth Cooper, in his July 1988 newsletter, quotes a recent Gallup Poll which says so. Cooper also believes that if the trend toward inactivity and obesity among young people continues, the whole wellness program is in jeopardy.

Other reliable sources report the same thing. For instance, in 1982 The Institute for Aerobics Research began a youth fitness program called FITNESSGRAM. Today the original plan has evolved into a nationwide program involving more than 3 million students and sponsored by the Campbell Soup Company. Where earlier tests placed heavy emphasis on athletic skills, the FITNESSGRAM places heavy emphasis on health-related measurements of true body fitness.

In the 1986-87 school year, more than 170,000 students were compared with a group tested in 1975. The results ranged from no improvement to declines in every event. The greatest losses were in the areas of body composition and cardiovascular endurance.

Another study conducted by the Public Health Service in 1985, the National Children and Youth Fitness Study, found that young people have more body fat and weigh more than they did 20 years ago. The study also found that at least one-third are not experiencing aerobic benefits due to a lack of physical activity.

Another study by the same group found a direct relationship between inactivity and fatness among those children having inactive parents and the number of hours children were allowed to view television.

What is meant by muscle function? Every muscle is designed for a specific task involving the body. Some are triangle-shaped like the trapezius and deltoid. Some have filaments extending outward, a little like feather fletchings on arrows, and some are shaped like spindles. The quadriceps and hamstrings help us to run and jump. However, the primary muscles used in running and jumping are the buttocks or gluteals. Not only do they provide a cushion for sitting, but they assist in standing and climbing. The most powerful muscles in your upper body are the latissimus dorsi. These extend from the hips to armpits and provide you with the power to throw an object or to swim the crawl stroke. The shoulder area contains the trapezius, pectoralis major, and deltoids. The trapezius assists in raising the shoulder area, the pectorals enable the arms to move across the upper chest, and the deltoids allow the arms to raise to the side and front. Another important set of muscles is the sternocleidomastoids. Located on either side of the neck, their function is to turn the head from side to side, and to nod forward and backward.

How many muscles are there in my body? Your body has approximately 600 muscles containing more than six billion microscopic muscle fibers. Even more astounding is the fact that each fiber is so strong that it is able to support more than one thousand times its own weight. The contraction of a well-developed muscle can break the bone it is attached to.

Then muscle use is very efficient in terms of calories consumed? Unfortunately this is not the case. When we do hard work about 75% of the calories consumed are lost as body heat. The heart muscle is more efficient, converting about 50% of its caloric fuel into effective work.

How can I make my muscles grow? Muscle growth is dependent upon three things. One, there must be growth stimulation within the body itself at the basic cellular level. After puberty, this is best accomplished by high-intensity exercise. Two, the proper nutrients must be available for the stimulated cells. Providing large amounts of nutrients, in excess of what the body requires, will do nothing to promote the growth of muscle fibers. The growth machinery within the cell must be turned on. Muscle stimulation must always precede nutrition. If you stimulate muscular growth by high-intensity exercise, then your muscles will grow on almost any reasonable diet. The third factor is adequate rest to allow the body time to repair cell damage and to replace the muscle tissue rebuilding ingredients.

Actually, the chemical reactions inside a growing muscle are much more complicated than just exercising, eating and resting. High-intensity muscular contractions result in the formation of a chemical called creatine. This in turn causes the muscle to form more myosin, which enables it to undergo stronger contractions. This in turn causes the production of more creatine, and around we go again. Remember, you must stimulate growth through high-intensity exercise and then provide the proper nutrients and rest.

What is my potential to increase my strength and recovery ability? While some researchers contend it is possible for an untrained male to increase his strength 300%, the average increase would probably be closer to 100%. Unfortunately, the gain in ability to recover approximates only 50%. Since women are unable to develop their muscular mass to the same degree as men, they will not be able to build the same muscle mass and physical strength. However, they should be able to approximate the same percentage of individual strength increase.

Why is weight training so much better at developing strength than just "playing" a sport or activity? There are two primary reasons why most athletes use weights. Weight training equipment allows you to isolate the muscles surrounding a joint and to work them intensively. This provides you with more results in a few minutes than you might get in a week of playing the sport.

I am more interested in developing bulk and strength. What must I do to accomplish this? Strength and bulk are best developed by increasing the weight and decreasing the number of repetitions.

Can I become "faster" by using a weight training program? Speed is usually increased with the development of strength. However, there does seem to be a limit beyond which an additional increase in strength does not improve speed.

Can I lose weight by weight training? Research indicates that men and women react about the same to a high resistance weight program. The lean body weight increases and the total body fat decreases. Unfortunately this does not do much to change the total body weight.

Most researchers agree that the most effective way to lose weight is by a combination of activity and proper dietary habits. Most also agree that a running or aerobic activity is necessary for best results.

How can I tell if I am losing body fat? Other than weighing yourself regularly, there is another simple way to determine if you are making progress in shedding body fat. The best way to do this is to keep a weekly record of the circumference of your upper arm or thigh.

Although most fat is stored under the skin with the thicker layers around the waist, when you reduce your bodily percentage of fat it is reduced proportionately from all over the body and not from any one spot. Thus, you may have a one-inch layer of fat at your waist and one-fourth of an inch on the back of your arm. As you reduce your fat and the one-inch waist fat is reduced by 50% to one-half inch, the one-fourth inch of arm fat is reduced to one-eighth inch. The difference is that you had less there to begin with.

Darden suggests the following rules for recording weekly arm measurements:

1. Take the measurements before a training session.
2. Use the same cloth tape measure for every measurement.
3. Relax the arm and take the measurement midway between the elbow and tip of the shoulder with the arm hanging away from the body. Record to the nearest 1/16 of an inch.

I have heard and read so much about "proper body fat" that I don't know what to believe. What do you believe? It is true that while most researchers agree upon a fairly narrow range, there is little agreement on an exact percentage. We tend to agree with Dr. Kenneth Cooper's recommendation of 22% fat for women and 19% or lower for men.

Can I gain weight through a progressive program of weight training? The traditional formula for adding weight through weight training is to use high resistance and low repetition. M. H. Berry in the early 1930s promoted the idea of using dead lifts, supine presses, two-arm pullovers and bent arm pull-overs to gain weight.

While most weight training experts agree that a few heavy exercises will promote weight gain but not necessarily an attractive body build, they also believe the best method of attaining the greatest development and physique is to add the bulk and weight and then to train down to desirable proportions.

I am an athlete and am not sure whether I am too fat or too lean. How can I tell? Most experts believe than an athlete who is lean and muscular should have a difference of one to two inches in flexed and unflexed biceps girth. Thus, if you have an excess amount of fat on your body you will have less than a one-inch difference. The leaner you are, the greater the difference.

Would "special foods" help me in my weight training program? Body builders are the world's worst when it comes to pouring exotic foods or potions into their systems. The only reason you should ever take special foods or additional vitamins is if you are not able to eat balanced meals, or if you are making weight for a sport and must stay on a low calorie diet.

If you had to recommend just one vegetable as being the best all around for dietary eating, what would it be? If you want to get away from calories, then a cup of chopped fresh broccoli fits the bill. For only 45 calories you get about 200% of the daily requirement of vitamin C, about 25% of your daily fiber needs, about 90% of daily vitamin A needs, 10% each of calcium, phosphorus, and thiamin, about 8% of iron, 6% of niacin, some potassium, and about 8% of your daily protein requirement. Not bad for a cup of one vegetable! Some researchers also think broccoli is one of the vegetables that may protect us against certain forms of cancer.

Is there a simple "rule of thumb" way to determine how many calories a person needs each day? You might try this simple guideline used by many people:

- Very Active — If you are a very active person you might eat 25 calories per pound of your body weight and remain the same weight.
- Moderately Active — You might need up to 20 calories per pound to stay constant.
- Lightly Active — A lightly active person might need as many as 15 calories per pound of body weight to remain the same weight.
- Very Inactive — A very inactive person will need only about 10-12 calories per pound to remain at their same weight.

Remember that while "total" calories are important, a "balanced" caloric intake is probably more important to all around total health.

Are carbohydrates particularly important to a person who is engaging in heavy exercises? Yes. The average athlete probably consumes 40-45% of daily calories from fat. Most trainers are now recommending that athletes eat about 70% (500 grams) of total calories in the form of carbohydrates. This serves two important purposes: first, it reduces cholesterol intake and, secondly, high carbohydrate diets are particularly important when training or competing on successive days.

What do you think of soup as a dietary means of losing weight? An excellent means. One study at the University of Pennsylvania found that when people ate soup at the beginning of a meal, the stomach filled which signalled the brain to curb appetites and slow the eating process. Other studies have found that dieters do better in losing and not regaining weight if they eat soup regularly.

How can I tell if I am suffering from a lack of iron in my body? A blood test is the only absolute way to determine iron deficiencies. However, we know that one out of every four women of reproductive age are deficient in iron with 5% being classed as anemic.

What about "extra" vitamins? Vitamins are not a direct source of energy and do not greatly contribute to body structure. They do regulate biochemical functions of the body and can be extremely harmful if consumed indiscriminately. If a person eats a balanced diet, "extra" vitamins are not necessary and may prove harmful.

What is a balanced diet? Most experts in nutrition advocate that each day's intake should include the following:

1. Breads and cereals (two or more servings daily)
2. Meat, fish, and eggs (two or more servings daily)
3. Milk and milk products (two or more servings daily)
4. Vegetables and fruits (four or more servings daily)

How many calories should I consume if I am a serious weight trainer? The intake of Olympic weight lifters approximates 3900 kilocalories per day, of which the major portion is carbohydrate. A high fat diet is not recommended since work efficiency from this kind of diet is not equal to a high carbohydrate intake and because of possible long-range cardiovascular problems associated with cholesterol.

What about protein supplements? One problem resulting from excessive intake of proteins is the increased need of fluids to convert these amino acids for excretion, thus sometimes causing dehydration. There are no super or wonder foods to improve strength. A balanced diet will do all that is necessary.

What have "body builders" contributed to strength training? Body builders have taught us how to develop the most muscle hypertrophy in the least amount of time.

After exercise, how long must I wait to regain my strength? Laboratory experiments indicate that if a muscle is fully fatigued it will take approximately 45 minutes for full recovery. Under ideal conditions, a muscle will regain 70% of its initial strength within 30 seconds and will be able to perform with 80-90% normal strength within seven and a half minutes.

Why should I do my weight program three or four times a week rather than every day? Research indicates little difference in strength gains between a three-or four-day program as opposed to a seven-day program. Also, the body requires a certain amount of rest for rejuvenation and growth.

Once I acquire the strength I need, what do I have to do to keep it? Strength can be maintained by exercising at least once weekly. However, all body parts must be exercised at a close to maximum repetition. It should be noted that this type of workout may cause muscle soreness.

If I stop exercising, what happens to my gains? Most research indicates that body conditioning acquired after a four-week training program is lost within two weeks if training is discontinued completely.

If I develop muscles and then stop lifting, will they turn to fat? No. Fat accumulates on almost everyone who eats a lot and exercises little. Well-developed muscles tend to lose size through lack of exercise, so the percentage of body fat and body muscle will likely change, but muscle does not turn to fat — the fat just accumulates.

How do women compare to men physiologically? It is generally recognized that strength in women is approximately 50 to 60% that of men. The male advantage is due to several factors including anatomical and hormonal factors, greater size, and less fatty tissue.

Endurance studies have shown that males have 10 to 12% more hemoglobin per milligram of blood and approximately 8% more red blood cells per cubic centimeter. Men have larger hearts and lungs, have slower heart rates, and ventilate less frequently during exercise. Women generally have 10 to 15% more body fat which does provide more load on the cardiovascular system and offers more of a thermal barrier to the dissipation of body heat.

This evidence does not indicate that women should not be allowed to participate in endurance type activities, only that males have a functional advantage necessitating separate competition for some competitive activities.

How do growth patterns compare? Prior to puberty there are few if any reasons for female performance to fall below that of males. However, beginning at about year eight, female performance on many motor tasks tends to lag behind that of males performing the same tasks. We do know that males tend to be stronger than females at all ages, and that the increase in strength is about the same until 11-13 years. At that point, males significantly increase strength while females maintain about the same rate of growth.

Males and females have approximately the same O_2 uptake until about age 12-13. At this point males tend to increase much more rapidly. Females do not normally acquire the same level of work capacity for males at any age, and the difference increases greatly with age. Until approximately 11 years of age, proportional limb length is approximately the same; however, after age 11, limb length becomes greater for males than females. Additional differences in running and jumping may be attributed to pelvic structure and the angle of the insertion of the femur into the pelvis. Body motion is sometimes described by positioning the center of mass. This is known to be lower in women, thus affording a more stable position for standing, running, and walking. It is well documented that men are generally stronger than women, and since the capacity to exert force is partially dependent upon the amount of muscle tissue at one's disposal, females are at a considerable disadvantage when competing with or against males.

What are the cultural implications of these differences? Play patterns of American boys and girls indicate the imposition of distinct patterns of play habits. Since this pattern has discouraged females from developing a strong sports background research is not complete in this area. However, the results that have been collected tend to indicate the following:

1. Females participating in competitive athletics over a span of years appear to be as well-balanced psychologically as those who have not participated.

2. The level of performance is generally not affected by the menstrual period.
3. There is no evidence that childhood competitive sports affects the childbearing function of females.
4. Psychological stress in well-supervised programs is not likely to be harmful to young girls.
5. Girls of masculine-type build tend to be attracted to athletic competition, probably because of the success factor. However, there is no evidence to indicate that participation in athletics develops or contributes to masculinity.

As a female, how much can I expect to accomplish by taking up weight training? Since women are relatively new to this sport, we have limited knowledge. We do know, however that female strength normally approximates about two-thirds that of male strength, and that females can respond to beginning weight training at approximately the same level as men. This means that women can significantly increase their strength by use of high resistance exercise.

Can I lift weights without becoming "masculine" in appearance? The opposite occurs. A trim, firm, well-contoured figure is usually found among women who participate in regular exercise of this kind.

Dr. Lawrence E. Lamb, the noted medical expert, states: "A woman can tighten her muscles and have attractive feminine curves with good strength (by practicing weight training) without fearing the development of what is classified as a more masculine physique."

As a female you have the same muscle properties as males; however, you do not have the same potential for developing muscular bulk and body size because of a male hormone called testosterone, which is produced at a higher level in males. Conversely, males lack the hormone estrogen which is produced at a much higher level in women than in men. Men or women having an unusual amount of opposite hormone in their bodies will tend to display characteristics of the opposite sex. It is not the weight training that does it.

What about the use of steroids? There are two kinds of changes that occur through the use of these substances: those that can readily be observed and those that can't. Most of the changes are bad, and some are irreversible. Those effects that can usually be observed among females are:
- larger appetite — can be reversed.
- decreased breast size — partially reversible.
- less body fat — can be reversed.
- increased sex drive — partially reversed.
- increased body hair — partially reversed.
- clitoral enlargement — non-reversible.
- behavioral changes — can be reversed.
- acne — can be reversed.

Changes that can't be observed are probably the most dangerous and include:
- decreased high density lipoprotein (HDL) and increased low density lipoprotein (LDL).
- high blood pressure.
- liver cancer and other degenerative diseases of the liver.
- decreased female sex hormones.

In males, there have been deaths. Impotency is also a common occurrence as well as male pattern baldness which is non-reversible.

I am more interested in developing muscular endurance rather than strength. What should I do? Muscular endurance is best developed by decreasing the weight and increasing the number of repetitions.

Can weight training cause a rupture? Hard coughing can cause a rupture. Anyone who is predisposed to ruptures can acquire one by straining. Actually, one researcher who collected information on weight training injuries found the evidence of hernia to be twenty times less among weight trainers than would be expected among an average group of people.

Can I become "muscle bound" by lifting weights? "Muscle boundness" refers to a limitation of a normal range of motion, and is possible when a person repeatedly engages in a movement that requires less than a full range of motion. It is also true that great muscle bulk reduces the range of any specific body movement.

There is, however, no evidence to indicate that a sound program of weight training will restrict or harm a person's coordination. What has been found is that each athletic event has a flexibility pattern peculiar to that event. Thus if restriction of movement occurs, it is the direct result of an improper training program which does not utilize a normal full range of motion.

What is full range of movement? This is a term coined by the Nautilus experts. They believe that a perfect exercise must be full range, including the following ten requirements: rotary movement, direct resistance, variable resistance, balanced resistance, resistance at the point of full muscular contraction, stretching, pre-stretching, positive work, negative work, and unrestricted speed of movement.

Are any exercises harmful? Some exercises should be used with caution and some others are not particularly beneficial to the human body. They are as follows:

Deep knee bends. There is some evidence that deep squatting bends may cause knees to be overly stretched with an accompanying irritation of the synovial membrane surrounding the joint. Knees may be strengthened by a 90-degree half squat.

Sit-ups with straight legs. This exercise is often prescribed to strengthen the abdominals; however, it is primarily an exercise for the muscles which flex the hip joint. If the abdominals are very weak, causing a hyperextension of the lower back, injury may occur. Sit-ups are excellent exercises, but should be performed with the knees bent and the feet movable.

Standing toe touches. Some experts believe that this stretching exercise may be harmful. The problem stems from repeated lunges (trying to touch the toes) with the knees and legs straight. Most problems arise from damage to the ligaments and muscles located behind the knee joint.

Is it possible to "black out" when lifting weights? Yes, it is possible. If a person holds his or her breath while pressing a very heavy weight, sometimes the weight tends to compress the chest, resulting in an increased intrathoracic pressure. This causes a quick rise in blood pressure and restricts the venous blood to the heart.

This lack of blood to the heart then causes a sudden drop in blood pressure, causing the lifter to feel faint or dizzy. This condition, called the Valsalva effect (named for a seventeenth century Italian), may also increase the intra-abdominal pressure with the possibility of causing an inguinal hernia. Do not hold your breath or hyperventilate, but try to relax and breathe in a normal fashion.

Is there a "special" way to breathe when exercising? Not that we know of, but it is important to breathe normally, allowing the demands of your body to determine the number of respirations needed per minute. Breath holding may cause dizziness, so do not hold your breath.

Sometimes I lose large quantities of fluids due to heavy exercise. What is the best replacement and is there a rule of thumb for replacement? Endurance events lasting longer that 60 minutes will benefit more from a diluted (5-8% carbohydrate) drink because carbohydrates delay the beginning symptoms of exhaustion. The general rule of thumb is to drink fluids equal in volume to that lost by sweating. Sixteen fluid ounces are generally considered to be equal to one pound.

What about steam and heat? Heat baths, both dry and wet, are not new conceptions. They have been popularized for many years as Turkish baths, Swedish baths, and more recently, as sauna baths and hot tub baths.

While research on short exposure to heat is limited, certain results of other studies dealing with dehydration, heat stress, and heat adjustment can be summarized to indicate what the average person might expect. Dehydration usually brings about a decrease in blood volume, with a corresponding circulatory deficiency. When you lose weight because of sweating, this is water loss and, consequently, is not permanent. Dehydrated individuals do not function well in high temperatures. They exhibit increased deep body temperature, increased pulse rates, and decreased work efficiency over long periods of time. More severe dehydration involving abnormal salt loss results in severe circulatory disorders manifested by fainting, low blood pressure, and weakness. This severe form of dehydration must be relieved by saline.

What about smoking and weight training? There is at present overwhelming evidence to indicate that smoking is one of the most dangerous habits engaged in by men and women. For instance, smoking only one pack a day increases the risk of a heart attack three times over that of a nonsmoker.

Smoking also seriously diminishes your maximum exercise capacity. McHenry at the Indiana University School of Medicine has reported that when a group of state policemen were divided into three groups and exercised to maximum capacity, the nonsmokers were able to exercise the longest. In this experiment subjects were classified into three groups: smokers, former smokers who had quit at least one year, and nonsmokers. Other findings were as follows:

1. Nonsmokers had lower systolic blood pressure levels than smokers.
2. Smokers develop faster heart rates at the same levels of exercise than do nonsmokers.
3. Former smokers had approximately the same blood pressure levels as nonsmokers, although those with previous history of very heavy smoking were not able to exercise as long as the nonsmokers.

It is a sad commentary that we continue to lose every year almost as many Americans from smoking as were killed in all of World War II. However, the national percentage of smokers has now dropped to 39%. Doctors who smoke have steadily decreased to about 21%. It is a slow process but we are making some progress.

What is a "burn"? Some weight trainers believe that if they can force an extra amount of blood into a muscle that has already been partially fatigued this will cause the muscle to increase in size. They attempt to do this by doing their initial repetitions and then following this with a series of fast half-contractions. This causes the muscle to produce a burning sensation, hence the term "burn."

What is a superset? When performing a superset, a lifter fatigues one group of muscles and then immediately follows this with a set for the antagonists. Although an extremely fatiguing method, and recommended for only experienced lifters, the method is considered by many to be highly effective.

What is a "blitz" program? A lifter on a blitz program trains five days a week but exercises only one group of muscles on any given day. Lifters who believe in this system recommend that each exercise be done for five sets of six repetitions each.

What is the purpose of the preexhaustion principle? The preexhaustion principle is a method of working a fatigued muscle even harder and beyond its fatigue point. This is done by doing a single joint exercise involving specific muscles. Immediately after fatiguing the selected muscles, the lifter moves to a multiple joint exercise that utilizes the muscles surrounding the fatigued set, thereby forcing the fatigued set to work far beyond its fatigue point.

How much should I be able to lift? This depends upon what your goals are. If you plan to enter weight lifting competition you should probably be able to power clean your weight plus 10-30 pounds. This should provide you with enough strength to clean and jerk 25-50 pounds more. If you should decide to enter a novice meet you will not embarrass yourself if you can snatch 10-20 pounds less than your weight and clean and jerk 10-30 pounds more than your weight.

If I "make a face" or jut my jaw will this help me to lift more? When you "make a face" your body contracts numerous small muscles in the neck and face. This wastes energy and increases the load on your system. It may help to impress someone but it doesn't make you any stronger.

How can I identify which muscle groups are involved in a given exercise? The easiest way is to read all the information included in this book. However, for any exercise that is not included, remember that the muscles which cause movement at a joint are usually located just above the joint and toward the center of the body. For example, when the lower leg is flexed or extended at the knee joint, the muscles involved are located between the knee joint and the hip joint.

If you have someone provide resistance to your movement you will be able to feel the surface muscles where the movement is taking place. Those muscles that are firm and hard are the contracting muscles and those that are soft and flexible are the noncontracting or nonworking muscles.

What about isometric exercise as a means of building strength? This method of exercise involves the static contraction of a muscle group when the joint angle and the muscle length remain constant. This form of exercise is valuable because it does not require a great use of energy and therefore the muscles recover in a very short period of time. A full range of exercise can be completed in a very short period of time and very little equipment is needed. While authorities feel that isometric exercises can be valuable to the beginning weight trainer and body builder, most feel they are of less value to the advanced student but can be substituted if traveling or if weights are not available.

What about using a "circuit training" machine like the Universal gym or others? These machines are very expensive but are becoming exceedingly popular in schools, athletic clubs, and spas. Actually there are both advantages and disadvantages so that a case might be made for or against their use.

Advantages:
1. There is no time lost in changing weights. The simple insertion of a metal rod will instantly adjust your weight for any exercise.
2. This type of lifting is probably the safest for a beginner since the weight is fixed on tracks, and it is not necessary to have a spotter to assist.
3. One of the nice things about using a circuit machine is that there will probably be other lifters working also. This will make

it easier for you to learn about weight training since every sport has its own vocabulary and weight training is no exception.

Disadvantages:
1. Advanced lifters who are quite strong complain that some machines do not permit a heavy enough lift. As an example, many of these machines have a maximum of 250 pounds on the bench press.
2. Some lifters feel that the weight is different than what it would be on a barbell because the balance is not true. This, however, has not been verified.

How about special belts that inflate, or rubberized airtight clothing? There is absolutely no evidence to substantiate that the wearing of such clothing causes a loss of weight or spot reductions of adipose tissue. Such clothing may promote sweating and therefore temporary loss of fluids, but it is the exercise that is beneficial. By all means avoid rubberized suits. This type of clothing can be dangerous in hot, humid weather. This attire does not aid in weight reduction, only in water loss which is temporary. The best clothing is that which is loose, comfortable, absorbent, and which reflects the sun in hot climates.

What about wrist straps? Are they helpful in lifting? Wrist straps have been around at least 30-40 years and it is generally recognized that they do improve gripping ability. The advantages and disadvantages are:

Advantages	Disadvantages
Help to better isolate the primary muscles for each exercise.	They are not permitted in competitive lifting.
Help prevent bars being dropped.	Sometimes offer a false sense of security.
Give a psychological boost.	
Allow lifters with faulty grips to lift more total weight.	Lifter sometimes "goes with the bar" when a lift is missed.

Is cooling down important? Dr. Kenneth Cooper, noted aerobics expert, suggests the following:

1. Do not go into a steam room or sauna immediately after working out. Wait until you have stopped sweating.
2. Do taper off gradually. Walk or jog slowly as this keeps the blood moving and improves circulation.

What is negative work? As you already know, when you lift a weight your muscles are doing positive work, and when you lower the weight, negative work is generated. Most authorities believe that it is impossible to stretch a muscle unless negative work is incorporated. Also, most authorities believe that pre-stretching is required for strong muscular contractions.

Aside from stretching, negative work will enable you to continue working a muscle that is weakened by injury or fatigued even after it is totally unable to do the slightest positive work.

What is so called "high-intensity exercise"? Most people consider high-intensity exercise to be the repeated performance of a movement against resistance which is done to a point of muscular failure. This means that you should do one set of each exercise at least eight but no more than twelve times. If you can do more than twelve, the resistance is not heavy enough, and if you cannot do at least eight repetitions, then the resistance is too heavy.

Why is high-intensity exercise the best method for increasing strength? According to Darden, there are three reasons why high-intensity exercise is the best:
1. High-intensity exercise produces better results with less training time. It is not uncommon to double a person's strength in less than a year using this method.
2. Fewer demands are made on a lifter's ability to recover; therefore, there is a greater reserve for increases in strength and growth.
3. High-intensity exercise is the safest way to train. "Training injuries occur when a muscle exerts a pulling force that exceeds the breaking strength of some part of the muscular structure. By performing ten repetitions, as opposed to heavy maximum attempts, the intensity is high and the force is low."

What particular kinds of body builds seem to enable physique builders and heavy weight lifters to do best? Most of the Olympic weight lifters tend to have a reasonably long trunk, big bones, thick waist, heavily muscled buttocks, and short arms and legs. Male body builders, on the other hand, tend to have smaller joints, bones, buttocks, waist, and hips. This is combined with exceptionally broad shoulders and an excessively large chest.

It is interesting to note that the Soviet Union encourages Olympic type weight lifting but strongly denounces body building as a decadent sport promoted by England and the United States.

Do people of the same sex have the same potential for muscle size? Sorry about that, but your potential for muscular size is primarily influenced by the length of your muscles, and you didn't have much control over what you were given. Individuals who are blessed with longer muscle bellies have a greater potential for muscular size.

What about body measurements? Carl Sandburg once said, "People lie because they can't help making a story better," and so it is when body builders begin to talk about their body measurements. First of all, it is important to remember that you cannot measure yourself with any degree of accuracy, since you cannot keep the tape from slanting. Also, measurements must be taken before and not after exercise, because a vigorous workout will temporarily swell your muscles. The tape should be of cloth or steel and you should use the same tape for successive measurements.

Where do I measure? A number of measurements are frequently taken by body builders and weight lifters. Those most commonly taken and the procedures to use are as follows:

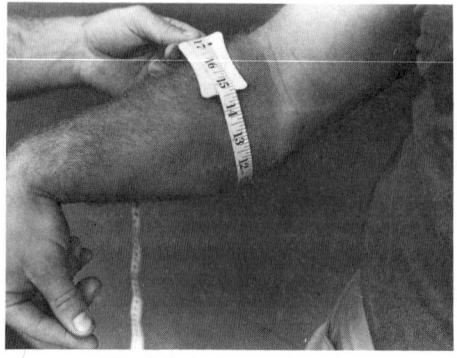

Forearm measurement.
Flex the arm so that forearm muscles are fully contracted, with the arm straight and pointing away from the body. Measure at the point of greatest girth below the elbow.

Biceps measurement
Bend the arm so that upper arm muscles are fully contracted. Measure at the highest peak of muscle.

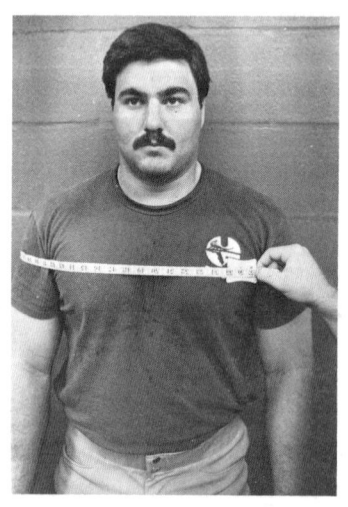

Shoulder Girdle measurement
Place the tape approximately one inch below tip of shoulder and measure entire circumference of body including the opposite shoulder.

Normal chest measurement.
The head is up and body erect with normal breathing; the tape should be placed slightly above the nipples and straight around the body. Be certain that the latissimus dorsi muscles are fully relaxed.

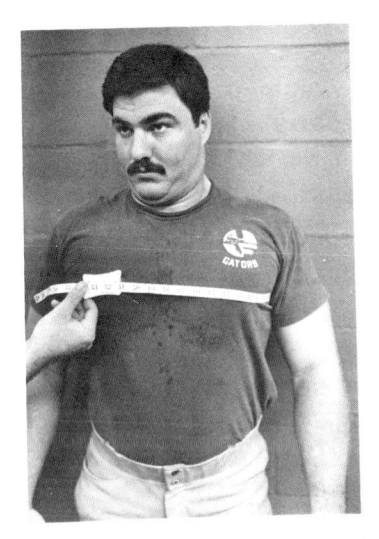

Expanded chest measurement.
Place the tape in the same position as for measuring the normal chest. Inhale as deeply as possible, taking care to not contract the latissimus dorsi muscles. If the expansion measurement exceeds the normal measurement by 2 or 3 inches, it should be retaken.

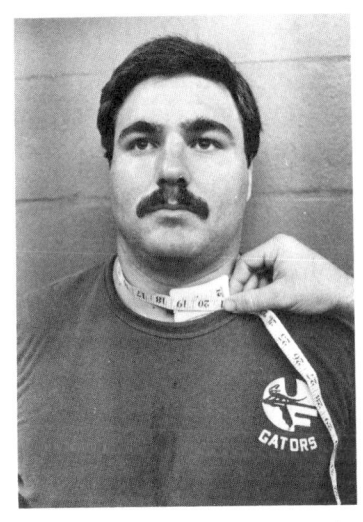

Neck measurement
The head is up, eyes forward and neck muscles relaxed. Carefully take the measurement at the smallest circumference which will be slightly above the Adam's apple.

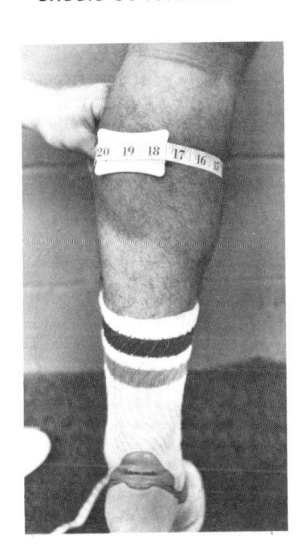

Calf measurement
Standing erect and with weight equally distributed on both legs, measure at the largest girth, or about four inches below the knee joint.

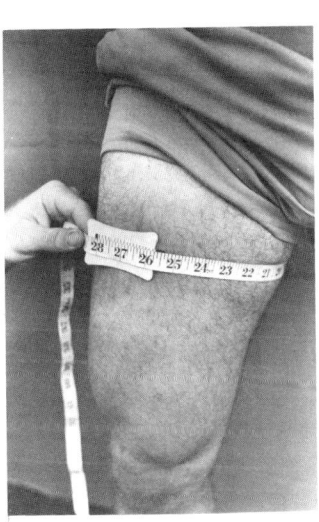

Thigh measurement
Standing erect with feet 6 to 8 inches apart with the thigh muscles relaxed, measure at the greatest girth.

Waist measurement
Standing erect and relaxed, place the tape slightly above the navel, and be certain to not suck in the abdomen.

I have read several books on weight training. Is there anything that weight training experts agree on? While there are many divergent theories on weight training, there is general broad agreement on several things. Most experts agree that muscular strength and growth are dependent upon:

- Stimulation of muscle by high intensity exercise to the point of fatigue.
- Rest — 48-96 hours between sessions
- Proper nutrition — a reasonable diet

Most also agree on the three principles of exercise, but not on the best way of achieving them. They are:

- Intensity — A degree of stimulation. Whatever that might be, it must be progressively greater than the normal workload of that person. This forces the body to adapt.
- Frequency — Or number of workouts. Most agree that 48-96 hours are needed to rebuild tissues.
- Duration — Somewhere between 30-60 minutes is most often recommended.

There also is agreement that both concentric and eccentric contractions are important. Concentric is the positive (tension and shortening) phase and eccentric is the negative (tension and lengthening) phase.

See Chapter Evaluation , Appendix D.

Chapter 4

SCIENTIFIC PRINCIPLES

An understanding of your muscular system is important in gaining the knowledge necessary to achieve your optimal health and fitness potential. All movements of the body depend on the functioning — contraction and relaxation — of muscle tissue. Although your cardiovascular system may be able to deliver large quantities of oxygen to the muscles, this will not ensure that the oxygen will be utilized. In addition to the functioning of the delivery system, the ability of the muscles to absorb oxygen from the blood in sufficient quantity to meet the energy demands of the activity is important.

When performing work, especially that of a continuous nature, the muscles demand a steady supply of oxygen to continue production of energy. The amount of work which one can perform and how long it can be continued are dependent on the amount of oxygen which can actually be consumed and, therefore, the amount of energy which can be created.

By learning how and why a muscle functions as it does, you will be able to plan more effectively a program for greater muscular strength and endurance.

THE MUSCLE STRUCTURE

Very simply, a muscle can be described as a band of contractile fibers held together by a sheath of connective tissue. Muscles attach to bones by means of tendons or fibrous sheets which stem from the connective tissue sheath. Ligaments are like tendons, but ligament fibers will stretch and they join bone instead of muscle to bone. The sarcolemma is the cell membrane of the muscle cell, and sarcoplasm is the more fluid part of the cell. Running longitudinally within the sarcoplasm are slender column-like structures called myofibrils.

The absorption of oxygen from the blood into the muscle cells is made possible by the presence of a substance within the muscle cells called myoglobin. Myoglobin is an iron-containing protein similar to hemoglobin. The myoglobin is also responsible for the storage of oxygen within the muscle cells. Once absorbed into the myoglobin, the oxygen then combines with the nutrients (fats and carbohydrates) and enters the mitochondria of the muscle fibers. The mitochondria are tiny structures within the muscle fibers where oxygen and chemical substances are brought together to produce a series of chemical reactions which provide most of the energy required for muscular endurance activities.

THE MUSCLE FIBER

The basic unit of the muscular system is the muscle fiber, and there are basically two types of muscle fibers. One type is referred to as slow-twitch fiber because it is slow to contract but has the ability to continue contracting for long periods of time. The slow-twitch fibers have a rich blood supply and high level of myoglobin and are important for endurance-type activities such as marathon running and long distance swimming. Because they have a high mitochondrial content, they are able to make good use of oxygen for the production of energy.

The second major type of muscle fiber is the fast-twitch fiber which is best suited for fast, short-term contractions. However, there are two different categories of fast-twitch fibers: fast-white fibers and fast-red fibers. The fast-white fibers are not as well supplied by blood vessels, have a lower content of myoglobin and mitochondria and, therefore, a reduced capacity for processing oxygen. These fibers are utilized in fast, short burst activities like sprinting and shot putting. The fast-red fibers have a better blood supply and a higher content of myoglobin and mitochondria which enables them to process oxygen a little better. They are used in activities of high intensity but moderate duration such as middle distance running. The fast-red are still not the equal of the slow-twitch fibers in usefulness during a long-term physical effort.

Each individual varies in the number of fast-twitch and slow-twitch muscle fibers in their muscle tissue. The particular ratio you have is determined at birth and cannot be altered. Therefore, it is clear that those who inherit a predominance of slow-twitch fibers have an advantage in the performance of endurance-type activities and a greater potential for the development of superior cardiorespiratory fitness. They will, of course, have a disadvantage in activities requiring speed and power sports. Individuals who have a predominance of fast-twitch fibers will not perform as well in long-term efforts which require superior aerobic capacity. Their potential for a high level of cardiorespiratory fitness is also reduced.

THE MOTOR UNIT

A motor unit is a group of muscle fibers. Each motor unit may consist of as few as three muscle fibers (such as the muscles of the eyes) or as many as a hundred or more (such as the thigh muscles) depending on the degree of precision required for the task. See Figure 4-1.

Each motor unit contracts as an entire unit. The reason for this is that all the muscle fibers in the unit are activated simultaneously by one motor nerve. If a delicate, precise movement is needed (such as in the fingers, eyes, or lungs), there may be only a few muscle fibers. When large movements are called for (such as in the thigh, back, or abdomen), each motor unit will consist of many muscle fibers. The nerve fiber with its branches and the muscle fibers stimulated by them form a complete motor unit.

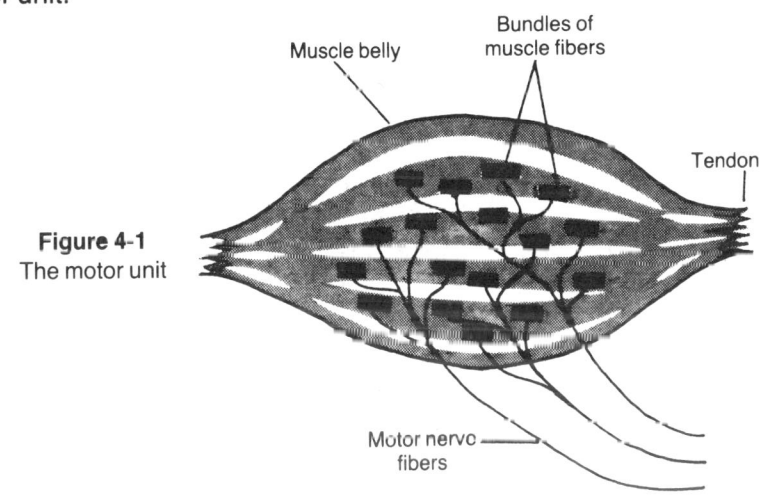

Figure 4-1
The motor unit

The minimal threshold of excitability is specific to each motor unit. The muscle fibers in some motor units contract with only a small stimulus, and some will not contract unless a very strong stimulus is given. A greater number of total motor units become activated as the nervous stimulus increases in intensity.

Whenever a muscle fiber contracts, it contracts maximally. This is referred to as the all-or-none principle of muscular contraction. Variations in the strength of the muscular contraction are therefore determined by the number of motor units stimulated. A muscle might contain numerous motor units, but the units may not all contract simultaneously. One factor is that the work load to be performed is evaluated in the brain, which stimulates the appropriate number of motor units.

Another factor determining the strength of the muscular response is the frequency of stimulation — the number of times per second that each motor unit is stimulated.

One reason a warm-up is recommended as preparation for strenuous activity is that when a muscle contracts repeatedly, the first few contractions are each progressively greater until the maximal response is reached. A weak muscular contraction can result not only if the muscle is cold but also if it is fatigued or the needed nutrients are not present.

The number of muscle fibers and motor units does not change throughout life. An increase in strength is due to the individual muscle fiber becoming stronger.

TYPES OF MUSCLES

Muscular tissue is much like an elastic band — it can stretch and return again to its normal resting length. Muscular tissue has extensibility and elasticity. The contractibility of the muscle is its ability to become shorter and greater in circumference.

There are three major types of muscles in the body:
1. **Striated muscle** — These muscles are the skeletal muscles of the body which provide force for moving the bones and stabilizing body parts. The striated muscles are composed of long, cylindrical fibers.
2. **Cardiac muscle** — This muscle is found only in the heart, and it consists of a criss-crossing network of striated fibers.
3. **Smooth muscle** — The muscles found in the blood vessels and the hollow walls of the internal organs are smooth muscles.

The involuntary nervous system controls the smooth muscles. The skeletal and certain other smaller striated muscles are called voluntary muscles. The cardiac muscle contracts rhythmically and automatically, without external stimulation.

TYPES OF MUSCLE CONTRACTION

There are three basic types of muscular contraction: shortening, lengthening, or maintaining a static position. Each of these is described below.
1. **Shortening or concentric contraction** — While one end of the muscle remains stationary, the other end pulls the bone and turns it about the joint. This is the usual type of contractor required for physical activities such as push-ups, sit-ups, and work with weights.
2. **Lengthening or eccentric contraction** — This is a gradual releasing of the contraction, as when one lowers a weight slowly. The muscle utilizes an eccentric contraction when lowering the body during a push-up or chin-up. The term "lengthening" is misleading since the muscle does not actually lengthen. It merely returns to its resting or original length.
3. **Static contraction** — During a static contraction, the muscle remains in a partial or complete contraction without changing its length. This type of contraction is performed when muscles which are antagonistic to each other contract with equal strength, thus balancing each other or when the muscle is held in partial or complete contraction against another immovable force.

However, it should be noted that not all muscular action is for the purpose of causing motion. In nearly every movement of the body, some muscles have other functions. These functions include steadying and supporting a part, stabilizing a bone to which another muscle is attached, or neutralizing the unwanted action of a muscle which normally causes several movements. Therefore, we can classify muscles according to the types of contributions to a movement which they make: movers, stabilizers, and neutralizers.

The muscle converts glycogen and fat into the energy needed for work. In order to burn these fuels efficiently, oxygen is needed. Oxygen is delivered to the muscles by the red blood cells within the bloodstream. However, it is not possible for a muscle to take in enough energy-producing food products during exercise to replace what is being used up. Therefore, your endurance will increase if you begin an activity with a greater amount of glycogen stored in your muscles.

EFFECTS OF EXERCISE ON THE MUSCULAR SYSTEM

As a muscle functions, the blood flow to it is increased through the capillaries into the muscle tissue. Therefore, depending on the type and extensiveness of the activity, there will be a temporary increase in the size of the muscle. Another effect is that additional motor units which may normally not be activated are called into action. A rise in body temperature is brought about due to the increased metabolic activity in the muscle tissue which increases the production of heat. The increased temperatures of the muscle cause the muscle to become more pliable, to be able to contract and relax more easily, and to contract at a faster rate.

Endurance exercises will also increase the production of red blood cells and stimulate the development of additional capillaries providing a richer blood supply to the muscle fibers. Studies also show that endurance training can increase the amount of myoglobin in the muscles and double the amount of oxygen that can be absorbed and stored. These and other changes can greatly improve the ability of the muscle tissue to utilize oxygen and increase its capacity for long-term physical activity.

REFERENCES

1. Clarke, David H. *Exercise Physiology*. Prentice-Hall, NJ.
2. Elrick, Harold; James Crakes; and Sam Clarke. *Living Longer and Better*. World Publications, Mountain View, CA.
3. Falls, Harold; Ann Baylor; and Rod Dishman. *Essentials of Fitness*. Saunders Co., Philadelphia.
4. MacLennan, Douglas. *The Fitness Institute Bulletin*. Vol. 3, No. 1.
5. Miller, David and Earl Allen. *Fitness: A Lifetime Commitment*. Burgess Publishing Company, Minneapolis.
6. Stokes, Roberta; Alan Moore; Clancy Moore; and Charles Williams. *Fitness: The New Wave*. Hunter Publishing Co., Winston-Salem, N.C.

See Chapter Evaluation , Appendix D.

Chapter 5

STRETCHING AND AVOIDING INJURY

One of the nice features of weight training is the almost total absence of injuries. In fact, when the activity is properly practiced, it probably has the best safety record of all sports. An added feature is that weight training will prevent injury in other sports by developing muscular conditioning for the entire body, thus causing you to be stronger, tougher, and more flexible.

PRECONDITIONING

It is highly recommended that during the first 4-6 workouts you use a lighter than normal weight load. This will permit the muscles of your body to adjust to new movements and will help to reduce any muscle soreness that might occur. This preconditioning period will also enable you to learn and practice the correct form for the various exercises before attempting to do them with near maximum loads.

WARMING UP

As your muscles begin to function, the capillary blood flow in the muscle tissues begins to increase. Also, a rise in body temperature occurs due to the increased metabolic activity in the muscle tissue. The result is an increase of body heat in the tissues which results in your muscles' becoming more pliable, more able to contract and relax, and better able to contract at a faster rate. One of the most important aspects of a proper warm-up is to engage in exercises that stretch the muscles and promote flexibility.

CAN STRETCHING PREVENT ATHLETIC INJURIES?

Although it has not yet been conclusively proven that stretching can reduce the risk of athletic injury, physiologic studies do indicate that it can effectively increase a muscle's compliance and extend a joint's range of motion. Studies also show that loading the connective tissue can increase its strength. For maximum effectiveness, athletes should perform passive stretches (with the muscle relaxed) and active stretches (with the muscle contracted). Techniques for passive stretching include static stretching, ballistic stretching, and proprioceptive neuromuscular facilitation. Active stretching can be done using concentric, eccentric, or isometric contractions.

Stretching or flexibility exercises have been extremely popular in the past few decades. We often read or hear that stretching exercises can prevent injuries and thus should be an important part of all warm-up training and rehabilitation programs. Many different types of stretching exercises have been developed, and each is touted as "the best" for increasing range of motion. Some of these, however, may also increase the risk of injury.

WHY IS STRETCHING DONE?

Several factors limit the maximum range of motion attainable by a joint, including the structure of the joint itself and the muscles, tendons, ligaments, and skin surrounding the joint. The main focus of flexibility exercises is to extend the musculotendinous unit to increase a joint's range of motion.

HOW TO STRETCH

A muscle can be stretched either passively (the muscle is relaxed) or actively (the muscle is contracted). Each of these types of stretching affects different parts of the muscle.

When a muscle is stretched passively, the portion of the muscle being worked (or loaded) is the connective tissue surrounding the muscle (the fascia, perimysium, epimysium, and endomysium). These tissues are referred to as the parallel elastic component of the muscle. Only if the muscle is passively stretched to an extreme length would the tendon be affected.

When a muscle is stretched actively, the portions of the muscle being loaded are the tendon and other tissues (such as the Z lines, which are a part of the actinmyosin crossbridges) that make up the series elastic component. The series elastic component transmits the force generated by the contractile element of the muscle. Thus, to work the entire muscle, both passive and active stretches must be performed.

PASSIVE STRETCHING

The three basic techniques for passively increasing a joint's range of motion are static stretching, ballistic stretching, and proprioceptive neuromuscular facilitation (PNF); variations on each of these have also been developed. Of these three, we advocate static and PNF stretching.

The technique of static stretching requires a slow, controlled elongation of the relaxed muscle; you feel a pull but no pain. This position is held for 10-20 seconds, and then the muscle is slowly allowed to shorten. Because the intensity of the applied force is low, static stretching presents little danger of damaging the muscle tissues. Yet, it can quite effectively increase a joint's range of motion.

Ballistic stretching is comparable to static stretching in its ability to increase a joint's range of motion. The ballistic technique uses rapid bounce to stretch the muscle; however, these uncontrolled movements can easily result in excessive loading and can damage the connective tissue by extending it beyond its elastic capabilities. Furthermore, neurophysiologic studies have shown that muscles reflexively contract if stretched ballistically, thereby further increasing the risk of damage.

One using the PNF technique first contracts a muscle and then relaxes the muscle while it is stretched. The PNF technique has been referred to by several other names, including the contract-relax technique and 3-5 stretching. The neurophysiologic theory behind this technique is that a muscle is better able to relax following a contraction.

ACTIVE STRETCHING

Passive stretching strengthens and stretches the parallel elastic components of muscle. Although these tissues are susceptible to injury, much more common are injuries to the tendon and its junctions with the muscle and bone. As a result, it is important that active stretching be performed to strengthen the tendons adequately.

Active stretching requires muscle activation during the movement: the tendon (which transmits the contractile force) can be loaded during all types of contractions; thus eccentric contractions are most important for active stretching of the musulotendinous unit.

An example of active stretching is lowering a weight against gravity in a controlled fashion. To lower the weight, the muscle is contracted eccentrically. Most people can lower weights greater than they can lift; lowering this weight, therefore, loads the musculotendinous unit with greater force.

DEVELOPING YOUR FLEXIBILITY PROGRAM

Flexibility is a very important part of weight training and all too frequently overlooked when programs are being planned. Flexibility is important for the average person because of its relationship to health and a person's working capacity. Short muscles can become sore muscles when exposed to physical exertion. In addition, inflexible joints and muscles can limit working efficiency and cause an individual to have problems such as those associated with the lower back.

Stretching exercises can increase the strength of the muscle connective tissue and thus reduce the risk of injury. For greatest benefit, all of the muscle tissues must be stretched using active and passive exercises.

To design such a program, the first thing you must consider is the temperature of the tissue being stretched. Studies have shown that an increase in muscle tissue temperature results in an increased range of motion because the tissue becomes less resistant to stretch. Thus, we recommend performing at least five minutes of active exercise (to increase the tissue temperature through metabolic heat) before beginning stretches. Exercises such as slow stationary cycling, slow jogging, and arm circling can help to elevate muscle tissue temperature. The exercises should not be done vigorously, but should be intense enough to increase the muscle tissue temperature.

Once the warm-up exercises have been performed, you should then begin passive stretching, with emphasis on those muscle groups used most in your sport.

GUIDELINES FOR A FLEXIBILITY PROGRAM

1. A brief cardiorespiratory warm-up such as easy jogging, running in place, skipping rope, or inverted bicycling, and preliminary movements of the skeletal structure such as arm circles and joint swings should be done. This warm-up is necessary to increase circulation and body heat for the tissues, ligaments, and joints, thus increasing flexibility of the muscle and skeletal systems.

2. Exercises must be performed for each muscle group or joint in which flexibility is desired.

3. The stretching should be gradual and progressive. It should be done with full extension and flexion being placed on the joint for a period of 20-30 seconds.

4. Stretching should be distributed rather than massed; thus exercises should be performed at least several times a day and four to five days a week.

5. Stretching should be gentle and gradual so as not to cause overstretching, since the stretch reflex may come into play, thus causing soreness and possible damage to the soft muscle tissues, ligaments, or tendons.

Questions About Flexibility

1. What are some of the things that affect a person's flexibility?

    Flexibility is associated with age, body size, activity, and gender. Inactive people tend to be less flexible than active people. When muscles are maintained in a shortened position, as the hamstrings are when sitting, soft tissues and joints tend to shrink and lose their extensibility. Also, excess body fat usually decreases flexibility.

2. Could I have adequate flexibility in one part of my body and not in another?

    Yes, because flexibility is specific to one or more body joints.

3. Which kind of stretch would be best for me?

    Most people believe there is less chance for injury by doing a static stretch. This involves holding a muscle at a greater than resting length for about 20 seconds.

    The dynamic stretch or ballistic stretch, which involves putting a muscle in a greater than resting length and then bouncing against the muscle, can be an effective way of stretching, but the accompanying side effects are frequently pain (cramps and stretch reflex) and muscle soreness. Unless a person is an advanced athletic performer or is working under supervision, it is probably wise to stretch the part out for 20 or 30 seconds letting gravity and the weight of the body part do the job

STRETCHING EXERCISES

Figure 5-1. Side Bends (1) With arms extended over the head, grab one hand with the other. Slowly bend at the waist as you gently pull hand toward ground. Repeat other side. 6 sec. each. See Fig. 5-2.

Figure 5-2. Side bends (2).

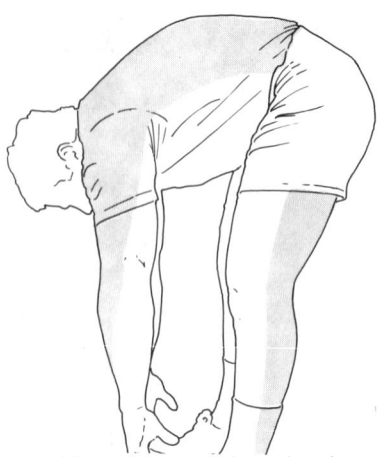

Figure 5-3. Toe touch. Standing tall with legs straight, slowly bend at the waist until you begin to feel a stretching sensation in the back of both legs. Hold for 12 seconds, taking care not to over stretch. Do not bounce. To return to a standing position, bend knees slightly to ease lower back pressure and to stretch the hamstrings. See Fig. 5-4.

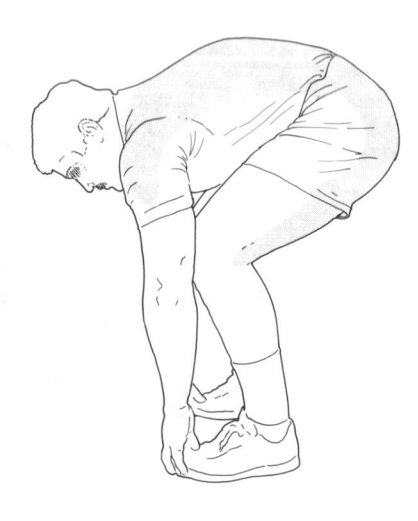

Figure 5-4. Toe touch.

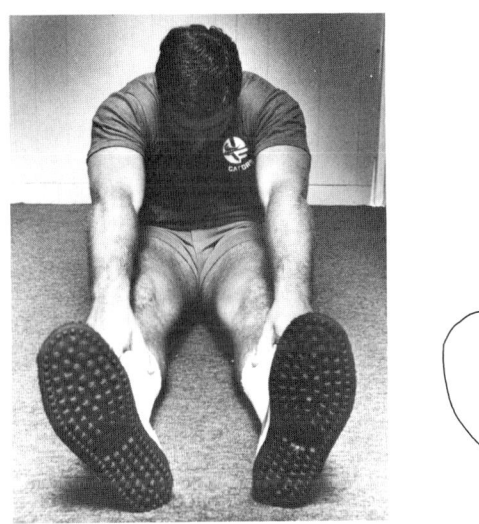

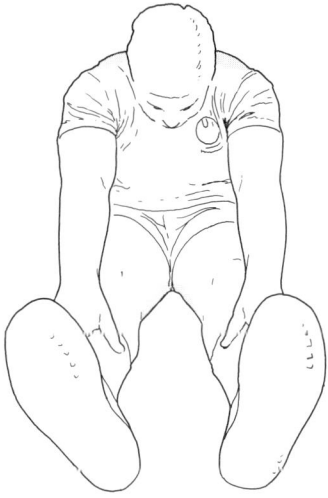

Figure 5-5. Sit with legs straight and heels approximately six inches apart. Reach at least to lower shins or ankles and hold for 6 seconds, then relax.

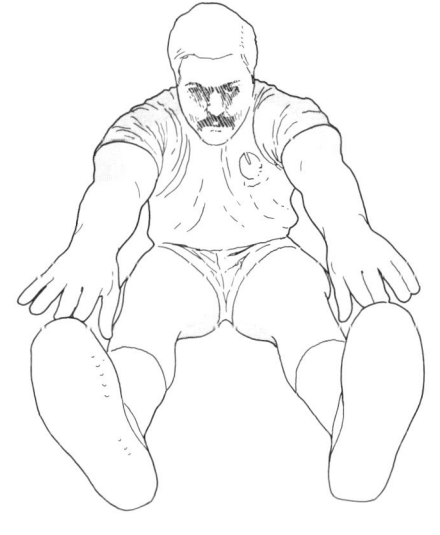

Figure 5-6. Phase two of developmental stretch. Touch toes and hold for 6 seconds, then relax.

Figure 5-7. Phase three of developmental stretch. Grasp soles of feet at instep and hold 6 seconds, then relax.

Figure 5-8. Twisting stretch. — Right leg over left. Left elbow behind knee — hold, relax. Left leg over right. Right elbow behind knee — hold, relax. 6 sec. each

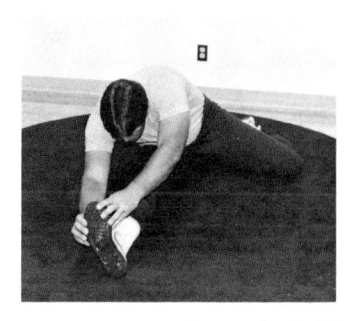

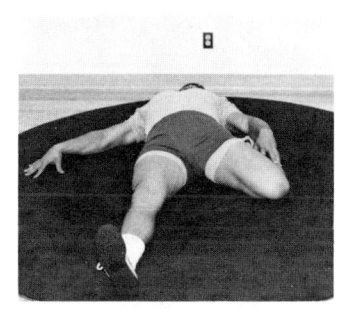

Figures 5-9 and 5-10. Hurdle Stretch

Purpose: Stretch hamstrings, quads, groin

Procedure: Start in a sitting position with one leg straight out, knee flat, toes up. The other leg should be tucked so that the heel is touching your buttocks. Lean forward, reaching your hands as far as possible. Grasp the part of that leg or foot that you can reach and pull yourself forward. Hold 5 - 8 seconds and lie backwards until you touch the floor or ground. While doing this, make sure that your bent leg is still touching the ground at the knee. Repeat.

Figures 5-11 and 5-12. Standing Groin

Purpose: Stretch groin

Procedure: Start in a standing position with feet spread wide apart. Point one foot out and the other straight ahead. By bending the knee of the foot pointing out, shift all your weight to that leg. This should straighten the other leg out. Hold 5 - 8 seconds and repeat to other leg.

Figure 5-13. Racer's Stretch

Purpose: Stretch legs and lower back

Procedure: Place one leg forward with the ankle directly under the knee. The other leg is straight back with the knee almost touching the floor. Now move your hips forward, keeping the front foot and back knee in their original position. Do an easy stretch on both sides for 6 seconds each. A stretch should be felt in the groin, hamstrings, and front portion of the hip.

Figure 5-14. Leg Stretcher

Purpose: Stretch lower leg and groin

Procedure: Pull your right heel to your forehead. With the right hand under the ankle, hold, then relax. Pull the left heel to your forehead. With the left hand under the ankle, hold, relax. Hold position 6 seconds each.

Figure 5-15. The frog. Primary Development: Ankles, Achilles tendons, groin, knee flexors, and lower back. The feet are shoulder-width apart and pointed out at about a 15-degree angle, heels on the ground, bend knees and squat. If it is awkward, support yourself against a wall with your hands. Hold stretch for 30 seconds. Learn to feel relaxed in this position.

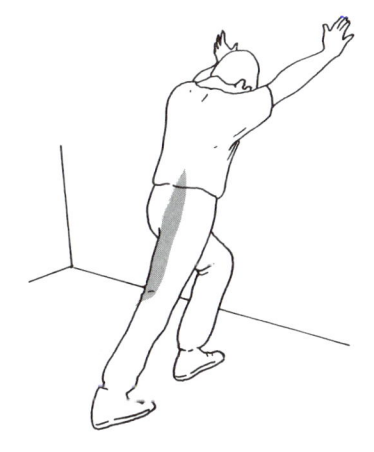

Figure 5-16. Hip rotator. Primary Development: fascia lata (outside thigh). Using the same position as assumed for the calf stretch, slowly rotate the hip out to the side, maintaining support with the relaxed leg nearest the wall. There should be a stretching sensation along the outside of the side of the hip that is not as striking a sensation as the calf stretch. Hold 15 seconds on each side of hips.

Figure 5-17. Lateral straddle stretch. Primary Development: for hamstrings, trunk flexors, and abdominals. For stretching the left hamstrings and the right side of the back. Slowly bend forward from the hips toward the foot of the left leg from a sitting position with legs spread. Keep the head forward and the back straight. Hold the stretch for 20 seconds and with repetitions the stretch will become easier. Repeat the stretch with the opposite leg.

Figure 5-18. Back lotus. Primary Development: for groin and hamstrings. Lie on the back, trying to be very relaxed. Bend the knees and put the soles of the feet together. Keep the body as relaxed as possible; keep mind relaxed at the same time. Hold the stretch for 30 seconds. Do not repeat too often while learning.

Figure 5-19. Single leg over

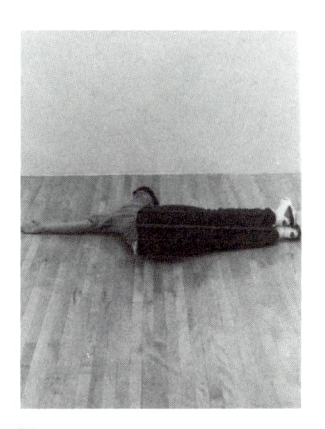

Figure 5-20. Double leg over

Single Leg Over

Purpose: Stretch groin, hamstrings, hop

Procedure: Begin by lying on back, hands out to side, legs straight out in front. Raise one leg straight up then lower to opposite hand. Hold 5-8 seconds then recover leg to original position. Repeat with other leg and other hand.

Double Leg Over

Purpose: Stretch groin, hop, hamstring, abdominals

Procedure: Begin as with single leg over. Lay on back, hands at side, palms up, feet straight out with toes up. Keeping legs together raise feet straight up and swing legs to right hand. Hold 5-8 seconds then repeat by swinging legs to left hand.

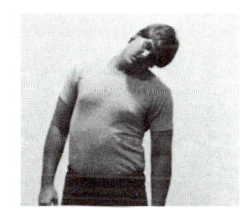

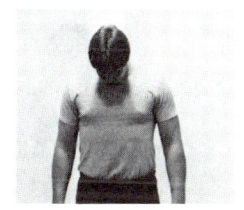

Figures 5-21 and 5-22. Neck rotations.

Purpose: Stretch neck.

Procedure: Primary development: Neck muscles. Standing with arms relaxed at the sides, slowly rotate the head in small circles in all directions while striving for a range of joint movement.

66

Figures 5-23 and 5-24. Spread eagle.

Purpose: Stretch hamstrings, lower back, groin, shoulders, abdomen

Procedure: Start in a seated position with legs spread wide apart and toes up. Lower the chest to the left leg. Keep the legs flat. Your partner will help you by applying pressure forward with his or her chest against your shoulder blades. Do not touch the floor or ground with your hands or arms. Once you reach your fullest range, hold 5 - 8 seconds, then force against pressure until you reach starting position. Your partner will then help you go down for the second time to an even further range of movement. Repeat this to the right leg, then between the legs.

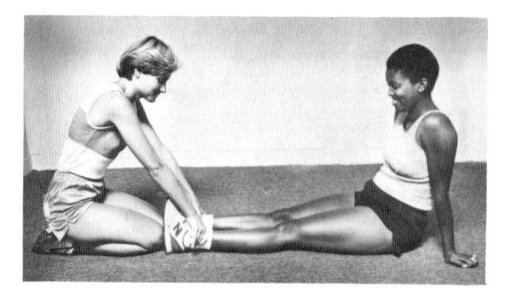

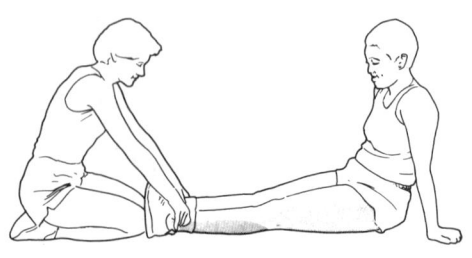

Figure 5-25. Groin stretch with assistance. Straighten partner's legs (See Figure 5-25) and very slowly stretch legs to a point of tension. See Figure 5-26.

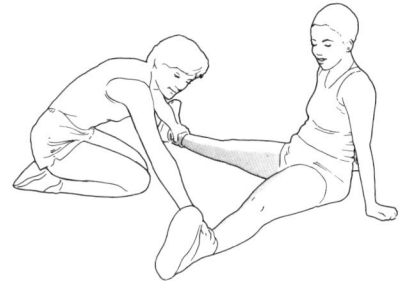

Figure 5-26. Groin stretch with assistance.

Figure 5-27. Yoga

Purpose: Stretch groin

Procedure: Start by sitting down and pulling the feet as close to the groin area as possible. Your partner will now apply pressure downward on your legs with his or her hands putting pressure on your groin area. Hold 5 - 8 seconds; then raise your knees up until they come together. Allow your partner to force them down again. This time should be further than last.

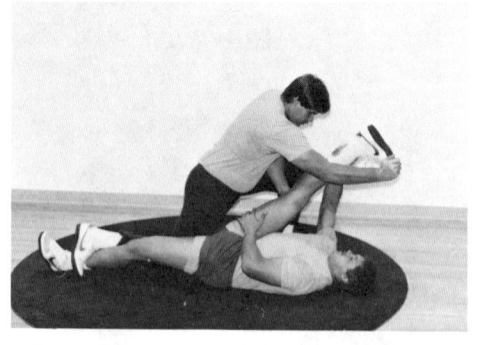

Figure 5-28. Leg Up

Purpose: Stretch hamstrings and heel cords

Procedure: Start by lying on your back with your legs out straight. Raise one leg upward. Your partner will then place one knee on your down leg to hold that leg against the floor. He or she will then place one hand on the toe of your up leg, pulling it toward your knee. Partner will place the other hand on your knee, keeping pressure on it so as to keep that leg straight. Now partner will apply forward pressure to that leg by pulling the toe forward. Hold at maximum range 5 - 8 seconds, then apply resistance back to the starting position. Partner again applies the same pressure to even fuller range. Repeat with other leg.

Figures 5-29 and 5-30. Partner groin

Purpose: Stretch hamstrings and groin

Procedure: Start in a standing position facing your partner. Place one foot in your partner's palm, which is held just higher than your hip. Turn your other foot to the outside (perpendicular). Lean over and touch your chest on your knee. Hold 5 - 8 seconds. Your partner needs to continue to raise your up leg as high as possible. Now turn your up foot in the same direction as your down foot and bend over, touching your chest on the other leg. Hold 5 - 8 seconds. Again, partner needs to continue to raise the up leg to the highest possible point.

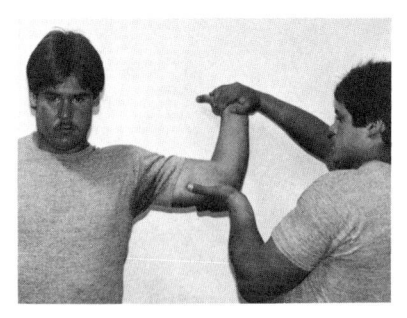

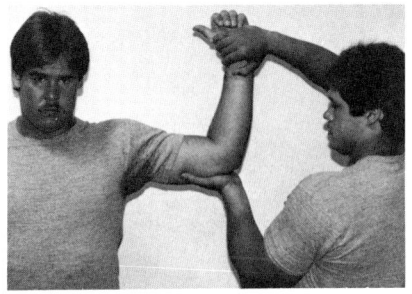

Figures 5-31 and 5-32. Rotator stretch

Purpose: Stretch shoulders

Procedure: Raise your elbow up (90 degree angle with ground). Holding elbow level, push your palm backward to the hold point. Resist pressure (2 counts) and go forward, then back again.

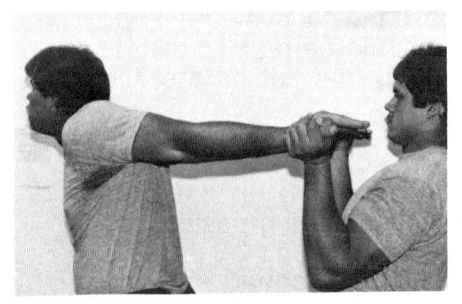

Figures 5-33 and 5-34. Palms down

Purpose: Stretch shoulders

Procedure: With palms down, raise your arms straight up from your side to a position level with the floor. Push your arms back so as to touch (cross them, if possible). Resist pressure (2 counts), then place together again.

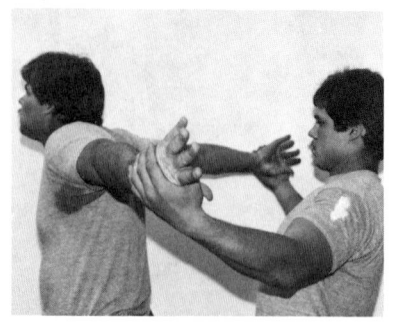

Figures 5-35 and 5-36. Thumbs down

Purpose: Stretch shoulders

Procedure: With thumbs down, raise your arms straight up from your side to a position level with the floor. Push arms back so as to touch (cross, if possible). Resist pressure (2 counts); then together again.

Figures 5-37 – 5-40. Neck curls, extension, flexion
(See next page.)

Muscles used: Flexors, extensors

Starting position: Lying on the back on an exercise bench, only the head should be hanging over the end of the bench. The top of the head should be parallel with the floor, arms folded across the chest, feet flat on the floor, neck muscles relaxed.

Action: Flexing only the neck muscles, raise your head forward and upward so the chin is resting on the chest; pause momentarily and recover to the starting position.

Spotting: Place a towel on the lifter's forehead and apply only as much pressure as is needed to permit the lifter to perform 8 - 12 properly executed repetitions.

Key Points:

1. Never exercise the neck muscles if you plan to engage in an activity in which head contact and collisions will occur (muscles will be weaker and more susceptible to injury). Stretch before the activity and after.

2. Never perform an isometric exercise for the neck muscles, for flexibility is reduced and strength is only gained at one fixed point.

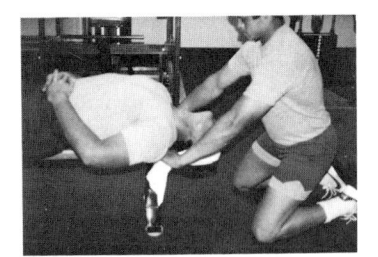

Figure 5-37.

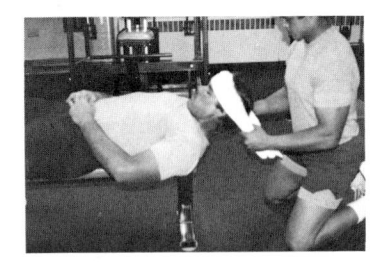

Figure 5-38.

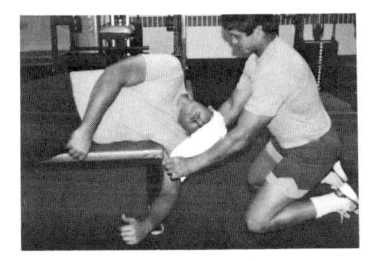

Figure 5-39.

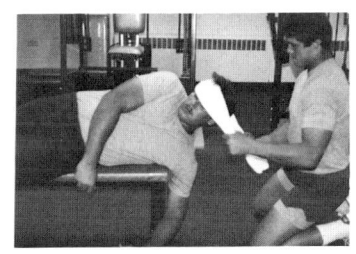

Figure 5-40.

3. Any neck exercise must be performed slowly without jerky movements.

4. You must adjust the amount of pressure applied to accommodate for the strength curve of the neck flexors. (More pressure should be applied when lowering the head than when raising it.)

5. The spotter should apply very little pressure when the neck is approaching the extended position.

6. The lifter should only move the head.

7. This is performed in all four directions.

REFERENCES

Clarke, David H. *Exercise Physiology*. Prentice-Hall, N.J

Elrick, Harold; James Crakes; and Sam Clarke. *Living Longer and Better.* World Publications, Mountain View, CA.

Falls, Harold; Ann Baylor; and Rod Dishman. *Essentials of Fitness.* Saunders Co. Philadelphia

Hubley, Cheryl; Kozey, M.; Stanish, W.D. *The Journal of Musculoskeletal Medicine*, Volume 1, Number 9. August 1984.

MacLennan, Douglas. *The Fitness Institute Bulletin.* Vol. 3, No. 1, 1980.

Miller, David and Earl Allen. *Fitness: A Lifetime Commitment.* Burgess Publishing Company, Minneapolis

Stokes, Roberta; Alan Moore; and Clancy Moore. *Fitness: The New Wave.* 2nd ed, Hunter Textbooks, Inc., Winston-Salem, N.C.

See Chapter Evaluation , Appendix D.

Chapter 6
BASIC FUNDAMENTALS

Stance — Head is held erect, the back is straight, feet are approximately hip width, toes pointed straight ahead and feet flat on floor. See Figure 6-1.

Grips — When grasping the bar, place the hands shoulder width apart and an equal distance from the inside collars. See Figure 6-1.

Figure 6-1. Basic stance

1. Regular grip — This is the most common grip and is secured by placing the palms of the hands face down on a bar that is resting on the floor. As you circle the bar with your thumbs, the thumbs will be adjacent to each other and pointing in a direction opposite to that of the other fingers. As the grip is secured the palm will be pointing back toward you more. See Figure 6-2.
2. Reverse grip — This grip is the exact opposite of the regular grip with the small or little fingers being adjacent to each other. See Figure 6-3.
3. Alternate of combination grip — This grip is sometimes used for lifting heavy weights and is secured by taking a regular grip with one hand and a reverse grip with the other. See Figure 6-4.

Determining how much weight — At the beginning, use enough weight to slightly overload the muscles. Although some muscle soreness may develop, maintain this poundage until the soreness disappears, then gradually increase the weights so as to keep pace with your increases in strength and endurance. You should experience complete muscle fatique somewhere between 8-12 REPS.

Number of sets — For the greatest gains in strength you should attempt to do three sets of any given exercise. Of course this may be impossible at first, however, do what you can even if it is only one or two sets. Within a very short time you will be doing three sets. One exception to the three-set rule is the bench press which should be done in five sets using the 8-6-4-2-1 progression. The Nautilus Company recommends a one-set total exhaustion procedure for their machines.

Length of workout — The length of time it takes you to work out will be determined by your lifting equipment, the number of people sharing it, the amount of rest taken, and the number of exercises and sets taken. Most beginners usually complete their workout in about 40-50 minutes.

Frequency of workout — Research has indicated that for beginners performing weight training lifts it is better to lift every other day or three times per week. Most experts feel that beginners need about 48 hours of rest between lifting days. An intensive circuit strength training program may only require two workouts per week.

75

Figure 6-2
Regular grip

Figure 6-3
Reverse grip

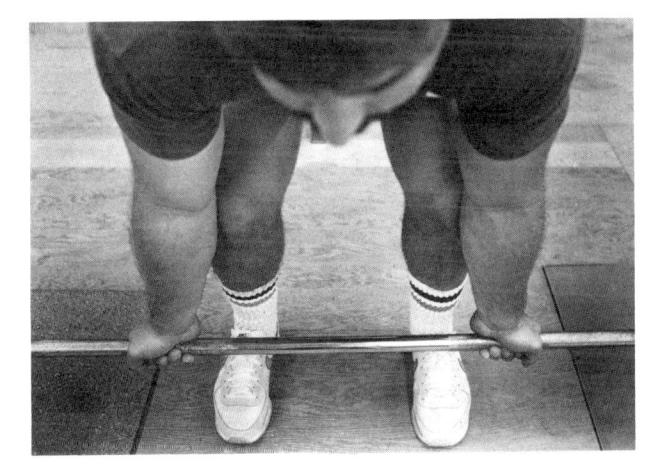

Figure 6-4
Combination grip

Dead lift position — Sometimes called the "crouch position" this lift is used when taking a heavy barbell from the floor. Please note that the back is straight with the hips lower than the shoulders, the head and neck are up with the eyes pointing straight ahead. Note also that the bar, hips, and feet are in line with the lifter's shoulders. See Figure 6-1.

Front thigh rest — In this position the bar rests against the thighs, with the lifter's body and arms straight. See Figure 6-5.

Chest rest — The bar rests lightly against the chest, with the arms under the bar and flexed. See Figure 6-6.

Overhead press — The lifter extends arms overhead from the chest rest position. Palms should be facing out and feet shoulder width. See Figure 6-7.

Shoulder rest — In this position the bar is behind the lifter's neck resting on the shoulders and upper back. The bar is grasped with the hands located just outside of the lifter's shoulders. See Figure 6-8.

Caution: Care should be used in taking this position. If heavy weights are being used, assistance should be secured.

Muscle length — The most important factor in determining the potential size of a muscle is its **length.** Thus, longer muscles have a greater cross-sectional arc and a greater potential for size. Untrained muscles that are disproportionate in length may be approximately the same size and strength; however, with proper **training** the longer muscle has the potential for being larger and stronger.

Figure 6-5. Front thigh rest

Figure 6-6. Chest rest

Figure 6-7. Overhead press

Figure 6-8. Shoulder rest

HELPFUL HINTS

1. Don't worry about impressing other people with how much weight you can move. This will tend to make you avoid certain exercises which probably are the very ones you should be working on. There also is a tendency to cheat on the exercise and if you do this you will be wasting time.
2. It is very important to control your breathing. Specifically **do not hold your breath,** as this has a tendency to cause dizziness or high blood pressure. Remember as the **weights go up the breath goes out.**
3. Your muscles need time to replenish and grow. Research has indicated that three days a week is probably the most desirable training schedule. However, if you feel that you really prefer to work out six days a week then you should probably set up two programs involving different muscle groups. Another suggestion would be to use one program three days a week and do your cardiorespiratory training (running) on the alternate days. There should be a resting time lapse of at least 48 hours and no more then 96 hours between workouts.
4. To increase flexibility along with your added strength, try to make your range of movement as great as possible.
5. Exercise larger muscle groups first, then work down to the smaller group.
6. Generally light lifting — less weight and more reps (over 10) — has a tendency to build muscle tone or definition, while heavy lifting with fewer reps (5-10) contributes more to muscle size and greater strength. "Heavy lifting" has been defined in many ways but for our purpose we suggest that you find the heaviest weight that you can lift **correctly** for 8 reps.
7. For the greatest gains, and to prevent injury, attempt to always use correct form.
8. If you cannot remain in control, reduce the weight.

HELPFUL HINTS

9. Keep the bar as close to the body as possible when moving it from the floor to your chest.
10. Keep your back as straight as possible with hips below the shoulders. This will prevent straining of the back muscles.
11. Keep your feet approximately shoulder width to provide balance and to spread the load.
12. Arrange your workout so that one area of the body will be utilized for the first exercise and another for the next. Advanced body builders and weight trainers sometimes deviate from this procedure.
13. Never squeeze the bar or machine hand grips tightly. Maintain a firm, comfortable grip since an excessively tight grasp may elevate blood pressure and use unnecessary energy.
14. Positive work or lifting should be on a two count. Negative work or lowering should be slow and smooth to a four count or twice as long.
15. Your complete workout should be within 12 exercises and take no longer than 30-40 minutes.
16. There are three variables in exercise, **intensity, duration,** and **frequency.** Of the three, **intensity** is most important in building muscles.
17. Avoid the full squat position, "deep knee bend" (one-half knee bends achieve good results with less chance of a knee injury).
18. Unless spotters are present, do not perform the "bench press" or other lifts in which you may be "pinned" if control is lost. However, if you do decide to bench press alone, **do not use** collars so that weights can be tilted off in an emergency.
19. Barbell plates should be properly secured to prevent slipping.
20. Keep hands dry by using carbonate of magnesia.

See Chapter Evaluation , Appendix D.

Chapter 7

ESTABLISHING YOUR PROGRAM

The first step in establishing an individualized weight training program is to evaluate the facility and equipment available to you. Because these items are so varied, we have listed a select group of lifts suitable for basic free weights, and for the two types of machines (Universal — Nautilus) most often found in training facilities.

The second step is to determine the type of development you wish. Chapter 7 is devoted entirely to tried and proven programs for a wide variety of sports and activities. If you decide to develop a certain part of your body, we have listed a Master Muscle Reference Chart with exercises to accomplish your specific purpose.

Most of the suggested programs provide for more than one exercise for each muscle group. This insures that a specific muscle will have a greater opportunity for size and strength. Remember that a muscle will develop more size or more strength only if it is worked with greater intensity or if it is worked longer than before. This is **overload** and is necessary if progress is to be made.

For a few exercises we have suggested two different kinds of REP/SET systems. The first is that of a pyramid 8-6-4-2 system, which permits no more than 8 REPS during the first set. Then the weight is increased so that no more than 6 REPS can be performed in the second set. Then 4 REPS and 2 REPS in the same manner. If you are able to perform more REPS than called for during a set, then increase your resistance on the next workout, so that the correct number may be obtained.

Greater resistance (more weight) and fewer REPS develop more size and strength. Another system which allows you to handle between 80-85% of maximum weight on every set and every REP is the system of five sets of three REPS. This system requires a good warmup, then set the weights with the idea of

Resistance — the hard way!

doing at least three sets of three REPS without undue strain. The last two sets may be adjusted depending on endurance. When all five sets can be done with the same weight or at least two have to be increased, increase the starting weight in all five sets.

Be certain that your muscles are properly "warmed up" in advance by the performance of lighter, exactly similar movements. When the muscle is cold, a sudden contraction could result in muscle damage.

All sets of a particular exercise should be done in succession before beginning the next exercise. It is very important that each exercise be performed properly. The correct position during exercise cannot be overstressed.

To use the Master Muscle Reference Chart
(Fig. 7-1)

First select the particular body part and muscles you wish to improve. Then, moving across the page, you will see the suggested lift for barbells-dumbbells; Universal Gym; or Nautilus. These lifts will be found in Chapters 8, 9, and 10 under the same headings.

Record Keeping

It is very important that you accurately record your lifts, weights, and REPS for each workout. To accomplish this purpose we have provided a number of tear out record sheets to record your progress. See Appendix F.

EXERCISES BY MUSCLE GROUP AND EQUIPMENT

	Free weights	Multi-station equipment	Nautilus equipment
Gluteal and erector spinae group	squat stiff-legged deadlift	leg press hyperextension	hip and back hip abduction leg press
Quadriceps	squat	leg extension leg press	leg extension leg press
Hamstrings	squat	leg curl leg press	leg curl leg press
Abductor group	squat	leg press	hip abduction
Gastroc. and soleus group	calf raise	toe press on leg press	calf raise on multi-exercise toe press on leg press
Latissimus dorsi	bent-over rowing bent-arm pullover stiff-arm pullover	chin-up pulldown on lat machine	pullover behind neck torso/arm chin-up on multi-exercise
Trapezius	shoulder shrug dumbbell shoulder shrug	shoulder shrug	neck and shoulder rowing torso

Pectoralis majors	bench press dumbbell fly	bench press parallel dip	double chest 1. arm cross 2. decline press parallel dip on multi-exercise
Biceps	standing curl	curl chin-up	compound curl biceps curl multi curl
Triceps	triceps extension	press down on	triceps extension
Forearm group	wrist curl	wrist curl	wrist curl on multi-exercise
Abdominal and oblique group	sit-up side bend with dumbbell	sit-up leg raise	abdominal rotary torso side bend on multi-exercise
Neck group	neck bridge (dangerous)	neck harness	4-way neck rotary neck neck and shoulder

© 1981 by Ellington Darden, Ph.D (By permission of author)

See Chapter Evaluation ; Appendix D.

85

Chapter 8

FREE WEIGHT LIFTS

HIPS AND WAIST

Side bends
(Lateral flexors, erector spinae, abdominals)

This is a very simple but effective exercise designed to firm waist, hips, and abdominals.

To begin, stand tall with a dumbbell hanging from one side. Now bend very slowly as far to that side as you can. Return slowly to an erect position. See Figures 8-1 and 8-2.

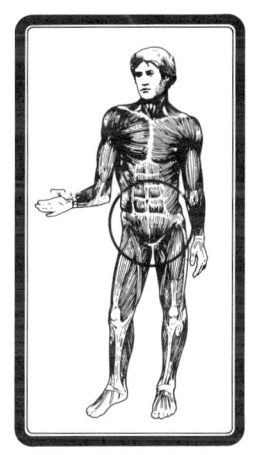

Hips, Waist, Thighs

Figure 8-1 *(left)*
Side bends I

Figure 8-2 *(right)*
Side bends II

Figure 8-3A and B. Twists

Twists
(External obliques)

One of the problems that frequently plagues middle-aged (and sometimes younger) men and women is the development of "Love handles" or fatty deposits along the upper hips and waist. Since the obliques are the muscles that twist and turn the body, it is these, along with the abdominals, that we must focus on. You will need two items, a bench that can be straddled, and a mop, broom handle or bar.

To begin, straddle the bench, back straight, and eyes looking straight ahead. Place the broomstick behind your neck and across your shoulders, placing each hand a few inches from the ends. Squeeze the bench just tightly enough with your knees to prevent your hips from rotating with your shoulders.

Now with your pelvis locked, twist your shoulders and upper trunk as far as they will go to the left. Without stopping, return to the neutral position, then twist as far as you can to the right. Start with 25-30 repetitions on each side and work up to 100 or more. This exercise may also be done from a standing position, but it is easier to lock your hips if in a sitting position.

THIGHS AND HIPS

Side kicks or leg splits with or without added resistance can be very effective in firming the sides of the hips and inner thigh muscles. In pictures 8-4 and 8-5 please note how a Number 10 food can has been converted into an inexpensive weighted sandal.

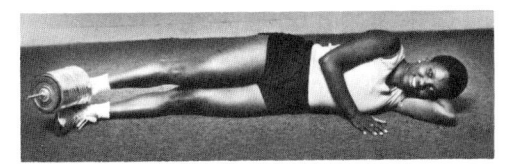

Figure 8-4 (top) and Figure 8-5.
Leg splits with resistance, I and II.
respectively.

ABDOMINALS

The best exercise for the front abdominals is the exercise that people have probably done the most—the old fashioned sit-up. However, there are some variations which will enable you to increase the resistance, but more of that later. To perform the basic sit-up effectively, do as follows:

Sit Ups

(Abdominals, quadriceps, hip flexors)

Lie on a flat surface with knees bent and feet close to the buttocks. The arms and feet close to the buttocks. The arms and hands are folded across the chest. Keeping the abdominals contracted, raise the upper body approximately half the distance to a full sitting position. Then lower to a position in which the upper body is not quite touching the floor. Pause momentarily, then repeat.

Key points: 1. The hips should be elevated to prevent the back from touching the floor; this will prevent the abdominals from momentarily recovering during each repetition.

2. When raising the upper body, do not come to a position in which the torso is perpendicular to the floor. This will allow the abdominals to relax and recover momentarily. (You should raise the upper body as far as possible while maintaining some tension on the abdominals.)
3. Allow the muscles, not momentum, to raise the body. Raise the body slowly while keeping the elbows stationary (4 seconds to raise the body).
4. It should take approximately 6-8 seconds to lower the body.

See Figs. 8-6, 8-7 and 8-8.

Resistance can easily be increased by lying head downward on an incline board or by holding a weight on the chest. See Figs. 8-9 and 8-10.

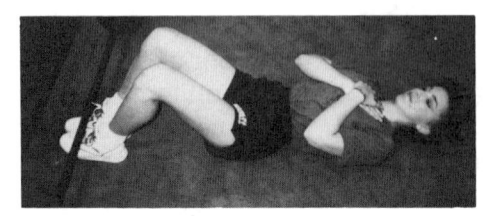

Figure 8-6. Situps I

Figure 8-7. Situps II

Figure 8-8. Situps III

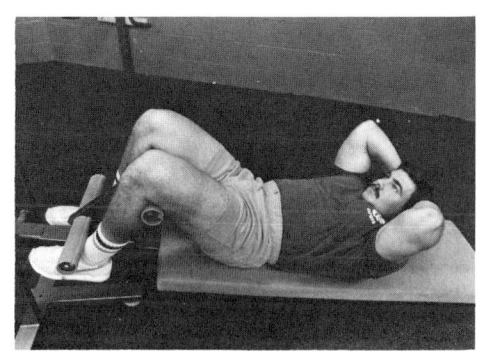

Figure 8-9. Situps I

Figure 8-10. Situps II

LEGS

Half squat

(Quadriceps femoris, rectus femoris, vastus lateralis, vastus intermedius, vastus medialis)

Squatting or doing knee bends is the primary exercise for developing leg strength and power. It is also highly effective for toning and firming inner and outer thigh muscles for women. One word of caution, however, most medical authorities have cautioned against dropping into deep squats, and for that reason they usually advise that a knee-high bench be placed behind the lifter to insure that the lifter's thighs approximately parallel the floor at the deepest point of the squat.

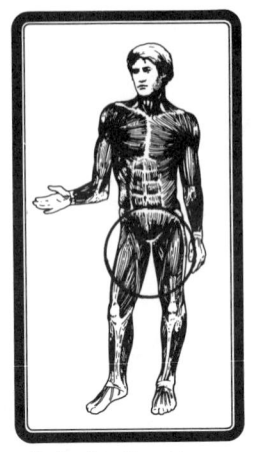

Buttocks, Quadriceps,
Hamstrings

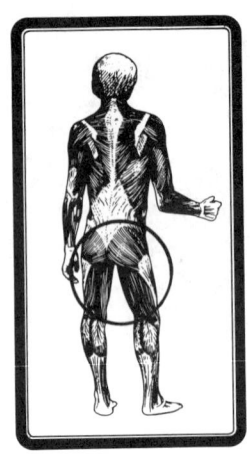

Buttocks, Quadriceps,
Hamstrings

Another problem you might have is keeping your heels on the floor as you sink downward. This is caused by very tight hamstrings and quadriceps but can be controlled by placing a two-by-four board or barbell plate under your heels.

To begin the lift, slide back and place shoulders under the bar (see Fig. 8-11) then gently lower so that the bar rests on the shoulders and behind the neck. If the bar is too uncomfortable as it presses against the neck vertebrae you may wish to wrap it in towels or some other soft material. Straighten legs to a full standing position. See Fig. 8-12.

Now sink downward, keeping your heels flat until the thighs are parallel to the floor. At this point your back should be as flat and straight as possible. Again rise until the knees are fully straightened.

Figure 8-11. Half squat I

Figure 8-12. Half squat II

One of the questions frequently asked by women is what weight should they eventually be able to handle in this exercise. While twenty to fifty pounds is a good objective, there is no reason why the average sized woman should not do squats with 70-100 pounds.

There are a number of top notch female athletes who do squats with 200 pounds or more.

Another problem is that if you seriously work at this exercise it will not be long before you will be able to squat with more weight than you can lift overhead. At this point you will either require assistance in the form of friends or a pair of adjustable squat racks.

To use these racks effectively you must set them at a height low enough so that the bar will clear the hooks when you straighten up with the bar on your shoulders. It also is a good idea to take a couple of steps away from the rack while doing your lifts.

Legs — upper-lower calf

Since there is only a short range of movement in the muscles of the lower leg, it is difficult to improve them other than running and walking. There are several exercises, however, which will increase the size and strength of your calf (gastrocnemius) muscles.

One of the most effective exercises involves placing a barbell across the shoulders or holding dumbbells in your hands, then placing your toes and balls of your feet on a short piece of two-by-four lumber. Now rise on your toes as high as possible and then drop back down until the heels touch the floor. See Figs. 8-13 and 8-14. Remember: bending the legs more will work the lower part of the muscle. Straightening the legs more will work the upper calf.

Another good exercise which works the lower calf most strongly is the seated rise on toes with resistance. See Fig. 8-15. To perform the exercise, place a pad across your thighs for greater comfort. Now place the barbell across your thighs and again use the board so as to obtain a full stretch.

For best results start with 50-100 pounds and work up to 150-200 pounds. Also remember that to work the entire calf you must change the position of your feet. Heels close and toes out work the inner muscles more, and a heels-out and toes-in position works the outer muscles better. Try to work to three sets of 15-20 REPS. See Figs. 8-16 and 8-17.

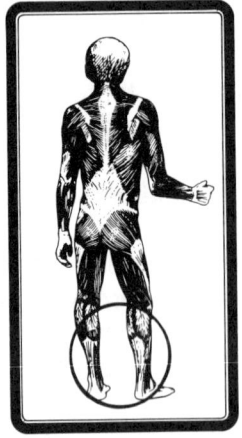

Gastrocnemius, Soleus, Achilles Tendon

Figure 8-13. Toe rise I

Figure 8-14. Toe rise II

Figure 8-15. Heel rise with weight

Figure 8-16. Inner leg muscles

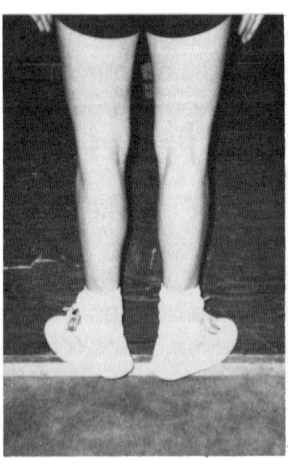

Figure 8-17. Outer leg muscles

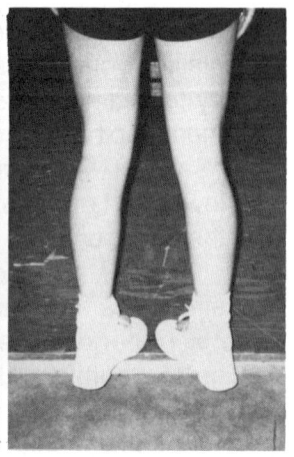

ARMS-CHEST

Barbell bench press
(pectorals, deltoids, triceps)

The bench press is extremely effective for the development of strength and muscle size for the chest, shoulders, and arms. However, a word of caution before we go further. Remember that if you have complete muscle fatigue the weighted bar is going to come down, and most likely it will be across your upper chest or throat. A few people have lost their lives doing this exercise, so it is critical that you exercise judgment as to desirable poundage and that you use a spotter if going all out.

To begin, lie face up on an exercise bench with the knees bent and the feet flat on the floor. The buttocks and shoulder blades are in contact with the bench, and the barbell is in the arms-extended position. See Fig. 8-18.

Now lower the barbell to the chest, pause momentarily, and recover to the starting position.

A spotter should assist the lifter into the starting position. If the lifter is unable to complete a repetition the spotter will assist only as much as is needed to complete the repetition. The lifter will need assistance when the bar is nearest the chest. The spotter should be bent at the waist with the hands under the bar.

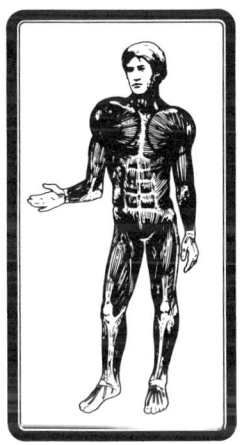

Pectoralis majors of the chest and deltoids of shoulders

Figure 8-18. Bench press

Key points:
1. The lifter should lower the bar to the chest with each repetition touching the chest at the same spot and maintaining eye contact with the bar throughout.
2. With the arms vertical to the floor, the barbell should be lowered to the chest in a straight line.
3. When recovering to the starting position the barbell is pressed upward and slightly backward so that upon completion of the repetition the barbell is approximately over the neck.
4. Dumbbells may be used to perform this exercise, especially when a slump has occurred.

Incline press
(pectorals, deltoids, triceps)

To begin, lie on your back on an incline bench with a barbell or dumbbells in the arms-extended position.

Lower the weight to the top of the chest with elbows touching the rib cage. Push back up with elbows driving forward and up.

Spotting: a spotter may stand to the rear of the lifter giving assistance when needed by placing the hands on the lifter's wrist (this will allow the spotter to assist the lifter in maintaining control of the bar).

Figure 8-19. Incline press I

Figure 8-20. Incline press II

Flying exercise
(pectoralis and expansion of rib cage)

Although it is not possible to increase bust size, it is possible to effectively improve the appearance of the bust by firming and strengthening the pectoral muscle of the chest, and it is an important exercise for women who wish to maintain a high bust line.

To begin the exercise take a supine (lying on back) position on a bench. Hold a dumbbell in each hand straight up over chest with palms pointing inward. Now slowly lower the weights, trying to keep the arms fairly straight. Be careful to keep the weights parallel since this produces the best effect.

Figure 8-21. Flying exercise I

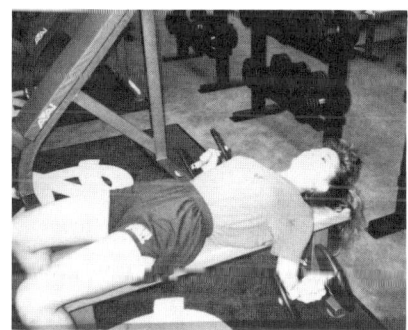

Figure 8-22. Flying exercise II

When you have lowered the weights as far as possible, slowly bring the weights to their original position. Remember: try to squeeze the chest muscles together as you lift. Also, the more you can lower the weights, the better the effect. See Figs. 8-21 and 8-22.

Concentration arm curls
(latissimus dorsi, rear deltoids, obliques)

There are a number of variations to this exercise, but all concentration exercises attempt to do the same thing, i.e., isolate the movement of a muscle or group of muscles as completely as possible.

Begin by grasping the dumbbell in your right hand and place your left foot just a little forward of your right. Then bend forward until the upper part of your body is nearly parallel to the floor. Use your free hand to hold on to something for balance, or place the elbow across your left knee for a stabilizing effect. The right arm and shoulder should be pointing straight down beneath you to the floor. See Fig. 8-23.

Now pull the weight upward to the right side of the chest by raising the shoulder and slightly rotating the torso. See Fig. 8-24.

Pause at the top of the lift, then lower the weight, rotating the torso back into its original position with the arm and weight pointed toward the floor. After fatiguing the right arm, switch to the left.

The high arm curl is another excellent exercise for almost all arm and upper shoulder muscles. To begin, assume a bent lunge position (Fig. 8-25) with the weight close to the forward foot. Now pull the weight almost straight up as in Fig. 8-26 until it is as high as you can lift it without turning the hand over and pressing overhead. See Fig. 8-27.

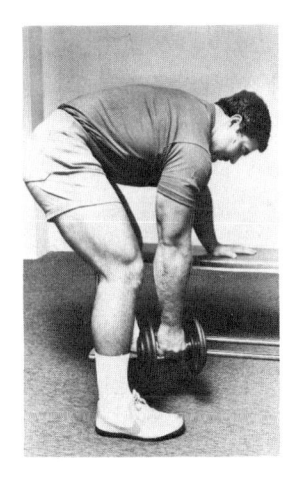

Figure 8-23. One-arm rowing exercise I

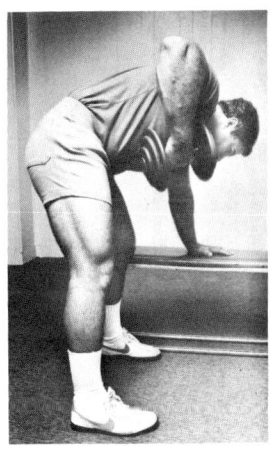

Figure 8-24. One-arm rowing exercise II

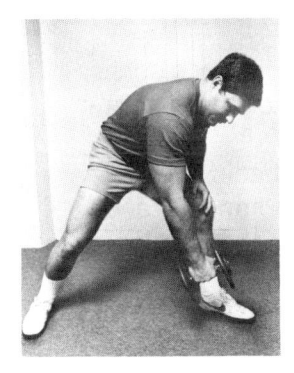

Figure 8-25. High arm curl I

Figure 8-26. High arm curl II

Figure 8-27. High arm curl III

BACK — SHOULDERS — ARMS

Behind the neck press
(latissimus dorsi, pectoral, biceps)

One very simple exercise which is highly effective for flattening and developing the upper back muscles is the behind the neck press. To perform the lift, assume a seated position and raise the bar overhead by utilizing a forward grip. Then slowly lower the bar until it is touching your shoulders behind your neck. One word of caution. Keep the weight well within your range and try to keep your upper back flat. See Fig. 8-28.

Latissimus dorsi muscles of the back and other torso muscles, including abdominals

Figure 8-28. Behind-the-neck press

Chinning is another excellent exercise for the latissimus dorsi muscles and, to a lesser extent, is beneficial for the entire upper torso.

However, do not be discouraged if you are not able to do as many repetitions as you would like to. Simply hanging and struggling upward will provide a beginning toward the development of these muscles.

As your strength increases, assume a wider grip on the bar with your hands as this will increase the resistance. Additional resistance also may be added by hanging a weight from a belt around your waist. See Figs. 8-29 and 8-30.

Figure 8-29. Chinning I

Figure 8-30. Chinning II

HIGHPULLS
(trapezius, deltoids, biceps, radials, pectoralis)

The upright row is a basic all around shoulder development exercise. To begin, grasp the bar palms down and hands close together. Lift to the front of your thigh and stand tall. Now pull the bar to your chin and try to keep your elbows raised as high as possible. Lower slowly and repeat. See Figs. 8-31 A and B.

One of the problems that many women and men have as they grow older is a tendency to accumulate fatty tissue at the base of the neck. The unsightly bulge sometimes referred to as "dowager's hump" is caused by the loss of muscle tone in the muscles of the upper back.

One of the simplest and most productive exercises is the shoulder shrug. To perform the exercise, simply hold a barbell or two dumbbells at arm's length and try to shrug your shoulders as if trying to touch them to your ears. See Figs. 8-32 and 8-33.

Figure 8-31A *(top)* and B.
Upright row

Figure 8-32.
Shoulder shrug I

Figure 8-33.
Shoulder shrug II

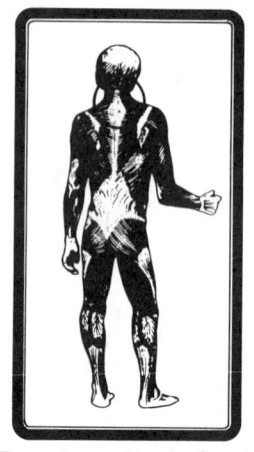

Trapezius and back of neck 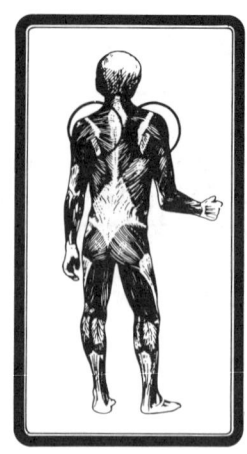   Deltoids and trapezius

ARMS AND SHOULDERS
Overhead press
(deltoids)

The overhead press is one of the most effective means of developing the front portion of the deltoid muscles.

To begin, grasp the bar with an overhand grip (knuckles facing away) with the hands a little wider than your shoulders. From a front thigh position (Fig 8-34), sharply pull the bar. With arms bent and elbows high, quickly snap your elbows down under the bar, thrusting forward and upward so that the bar will be resting on the palms at chest level. A slight knee dip will allow you to better bring your hips under the bar and will cushion the impact of the bar when it comes to rest against the upper chest (Fig 8-35).

At this point, thrust the hips slightly forward, tensing thighs, buttocks, and low back muscles as you push the weighted bar smoothly overhead. Try to keep the bar as close to your face as possible and move forward slightly so that as the bar clears the top of your head, your arms and body will be directly under the weight (Fig 8-36). Remember to take a breath before pressing the weights upward and then exhale as the arms straighten and inhale as you lower to begin another Rep.

The dumbbell press is a variation of the barbell press and is an excellent means of working the shoulders and arms equally. It also is an excellent way to firm the chest area above the bust.

Since the exercise is performed more effectively from an inclined bench, lie back on the board with two dumbbells that you can adequately handle. (See figs. 8-37 and 8-38). Now

Figure 8-34 *(left).*
Overhead press I

Figure 8-35 *(below left).*
Overhead press II

Figure 8-36 *(below right).*
Overhead press III

Figure 8-37 *(left).*
Overhead press I

Figure 8-38 *(right).*
Overhead press II

push the weights toward the ceiling, trying to fully extend the arms. To completely work all muscles involved, try to extend as shown in the pictures, but also extend so that the dumbbells are pointing toward your ears when the arms are fully locked.

Note: Remember to take twice as much time to lower as to raise, and blow the weights up.

Figure 8-39. Sitting press I

Figure 8-40. Sitting press II

Sitting Press
(latissimus dorsi, pectorals, biceps, triceps)

Begin the sitting press by holding the weight over your head. Now lower the weight behind your head until it touches your neck. As soon as it touches, push the weight up to arms length. A spotter is recommended for this lift.

Figure 8-41. Forward back bends

Lower back

LOWER BACK

Forward bends

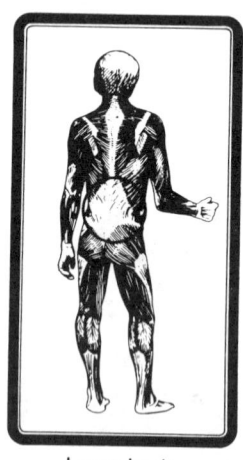

Trimming and firming the lower back muscles is exceedingly difficult for many people because of a proneness to lower back strains or past injuries to the lower back. If you are a person with these problems, please be particularly careful to use very light weights and bend forward **only until you feel a comfortable stretch in your back muscles.**

To begin, place a very light weight across your shoulders and bend your knees slightly. Then bend forward at the waist until you begin to feel an easy stretch and straighten to a standing-tall position prior to the next Rep. A backward lean and shoulder shrug as you straighten up will help to loosen your muscles and make you feel more comfortable. See Fig. 8-41.

Bent lateral raises
(back deltoids)

One of the problems with most arm exercises is that the front and sides of the deltoids are usually worked quite well, but the rear part at the back of the shoulders may receive little or no attention.

To achieve the desired effect, we must lean well forward to an angle of about 50-80 degrees. Now, keeping your arms nearly straight, raise a pair of dumbbells to the sides as high as you can and return as slowly as possible to their original position. See Figs. 8-42 and 8-43.

Figure 8-42.

Figure 8-43.

ARMS
Lateral raises

The lateral raise is an excellent exercise for developing the sides of your shoulders. Because you should keep your arms almost straight, it will be very difficult to do this exercise with more than 10-20 pounds in each hand.

Grasp a light dumbbell in each hand. With arms hanging loosely and knuckles pointing away from your body, raise the weights sideways until they are fully overhead. Then return very slowly to the original position. See Figs. 8-42 — 8-46.

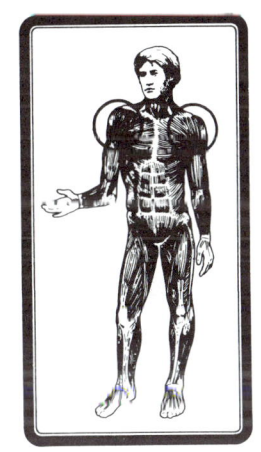

Deltoids

Stifflegged dead lift
(lowerback, hamstrings, buttocks, calves)

Place feet shoulder-width apart on platform. Grasp dumbbells with knuckles pointing outward and slowly bend at the waist to the lowest possible depth. Hang a few seconds and return to the starting position.

Key Points:
* never bounce
* lower weights slowly
* keep legs locked
* if weight touches floor, increase platform height.

Figure 8-44.  **Figure 8-45.**

For a more effective exercise try to keep the dumbbells tilted downwards at the front ends. Be sure to spread your legs slightly for a good supporting base, and try to stand tall.

Side lateral raise

Standing with the arms extended downward, palms facing each other with the dumbbells touching in front of the body, the body is slightly bent forward at the waist.

Raise the dumbbells sideward and upward so that the dumbbells are approximately parallel with the head; pause momentarily and recover to the starting position. Raise one arm at a time.

Figure 8-46.
Side lateral raise

Frontal raise
(deltoids)

To begin this lift, stand tall, with the weight in your lifting hand. Raise one arm at a time. The arm should be contracting inward as the weight is raised. Fist and elbow should raise to chin height and on a level plane. Be sure arms are fully extended on the lowering phase.

Figure 8-47.
Frontal raise I

Figure 8-48.
Frontal raise II

Two-arm curls
(biceps, radialis, brachioradialis)

Front curl — This is the traditional "show me your muscle" exercise, and the best way to develop it is as follows. Assume a comfortable stance with the bar resting across the thighs. You should have an underhand grip (palms pointing outward at hip width), then slowly flex your arms bringing the bar to your chest. Take special care to prevent the elbows from moving backward. Also try to keep from leaning backward and swinging the weights to chest level. Remember to lower the bar slowly and to fully extend the elbows before repeating the movement. See Figs. 8-49 and 8 50.

Reverse curl — The reverse curl is performed in the same manner as the front curl except the palms are turned inward rather than outward. Reverse curls work the forearms very strongly and because of this you will probably be able to handle less weight than in the front curl. See Figs. 8-51 and 8-52.

One arm concentration curls — This is another excellent arm exercise. Begin by placing one elbow firmly against your leg. See Fig. 8-53. Now flex the arm taking care to maintain arm-elbow contact with your leg at all times. See Fig. 8-54. Another popular variation is to stand behind an incline board with the upper arm and elbow resting on the board at all times.

Figure 8-49. Two-arm curl I    **Figure 8-50.** Two-arm curl II

Figure 8-51. Reverse curl I    **Figure 8-52.** Reverse curl II

Figure 8-53. Concentration curl I    **Figure 8-54.** Concentration curl II

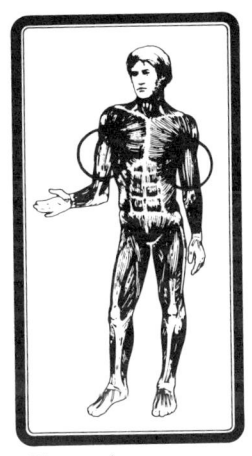

Biceps of upper arms

UPPER ARM

Triceps extension
(triceps)

Try this simple exercise for sagging or flabby upper arm muscles. To begin, lift a dumbbell above your head, keeping your elbow in close to your head. Now bend your elbow very slowly, lowering the weighted hand behind your head until the weights touch your back. Still keeping the elbow in close to your head, straighten the arm, returning the dumbbell to its original overhead position. See Figs. 8-55 and 8-56. **CAUTION:** Be careful! As the arm becomes fatigued there is a tendency to bump yourself on the head with the weights.

Triceps extensions
(triceps)

These two exercises, sometimes called a French press or triceps press, are excellent for strengthening and firming the back or under portion of the arm. One word of caution, do not overload excessively as this exercise has a reputation for causing sore elbows and some people may find that their bodies cannot adapt to this particular exercise.

To begin, place your hands about 8-12 inches apart and press a light barbell over your head. Keeping your elbows as close together as possible, lower the weight behind your head.

Figure 8-55 *(left).*
Triceps extension I

Figure 8-56 *(right).*
Triceps extension II

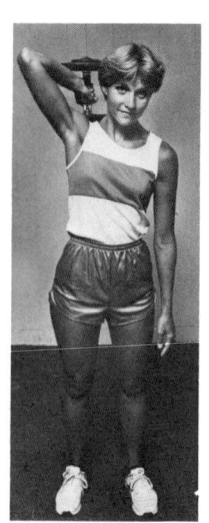

Try to keep the elbows perpendicular or straight up, using them as a hinge for the movement. See Figs 8-57 and 8-58.

A variation of this exercise is often performed by lying flat on a bench, extending the weight overhead and then lowering as described above.

Figure 8-57.
Triceps press I

Figure 8-58.
Triceps press II

FOREARM-WRIST-FINGERS
Wrist curls

Almost all sports rely heavily on forearms, wrist, and finger strength. Begin the exercise by picking the barbell or dumbbells up with an underhand grip (see picture) with the hands less than shoulder width apart. Sit on a bench and extend the hands beyond the knees with the forearms supported on your thighs. Now raise and lower the weight by moving hands, wrists, and fingers only. One word of caution, if you do the exercise too fast the bar may roll past the fingertips and hit the floor. See the figures below.

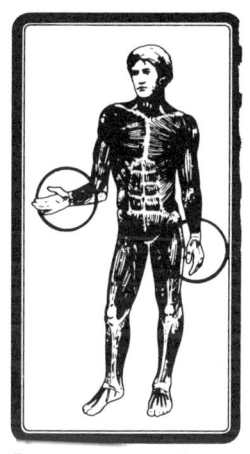

Forearms, wrists, fingers

Figure 8-59.

Figure 8-60.

Figure 8-61.

Figure 8-62.

Figure 8-63 *(left)*. Reverse wrist curl I
Figure 8-64 *(right)*. Reverse wrist curl II

The reverse wrist curl

This exercise uses an overhand grip, with the thumbs toward the center of the bar and the knuckles pointing up and away. This exercise removes the biceps muscles and forces the greater effort from the forearm muscles. See Figs. 8-63 and 8-64.

Pronated wrist curls

This is an excellent exercise for an person who plays a racquet sport. To begin, grasp the dumbbell at one extreme end and allow it to point downward toward the floor. Now slowly raise the lower end until it is pointing almost directly upward. Repeat 10-12 REPS. See Figs. 8-65 and 8-66.

Figure 8-65.
Pronated wrist curls I

Figure 8-66.
Pronated wrist curls II

Rotation of neck and head to right and left

Wrestler's bridge

The wrestler's bridge is so named because it is a primary defense of wrestlers to prevent having their shoulders pinned to the mat. However, it is also an excellent exercise to condition and strengthen neck muscles for any activity.

To do the exercise, secure something to use as padding for your head. Place the pad on the floor and lie on your back with the tip of your head resting on the near edge of the pad. Now pull your feet in close to your buttocks and inch your body up until you are supported at only two points, head and feet. (See Fig. 8-67).

Increased flexibility may be obtained by using the head as a pivot point and working the feet sideward so that your body moves in a full circle with the head as pivot.

Additional resistance is obtained by holding a five- or ten-pound weight on your chest while doing this exercise.

While many sports trainers use this exercise to strengthen the neck muscles *CAUTION IS ADVISED.*

Figure 8-67. Wrestler's bridge

See Chapter Evaluation , Appendix D.

Chapter 9

THE UNIVERSAL MACHINE

LEGS

Universal — regular leg press
1. Lower foot position pedals.
2. Extend legs fully so that knees are straight.
3. Slowly return to flexed position with weight under control.

Universal — calf, ankle, arch press
1. Lower foot position pedals.
2. Extend legs fully, pressing with toes and ball of foot.
3. When knees are straight, extend arches and toes as far as possible.
4. Repeat movement.

Figure 9-1. Leg press I

Figure 9-2. Leg press II

Figure 9-3. Leg extension I

Figure 9-4. Leg extension II

Universal — leg extension
(quadriceps)
1. Sit upright on table.
2. Place top of foot below the roller.
3. Hold on to the table with both hands and lift both legs together.
4. When fully extended, flex both thighs.
5. Lower weight very slowly to starting position.

Universal — leg curl
(hamstrings)
1. Assume standing position with hands on grips.
2. Place heel under roller with knees pointing straight ahead.
3. Pull heel as far as possible toward buttocks.
4. **Slowly** return to original position.

Figure 9-5. Leg curl

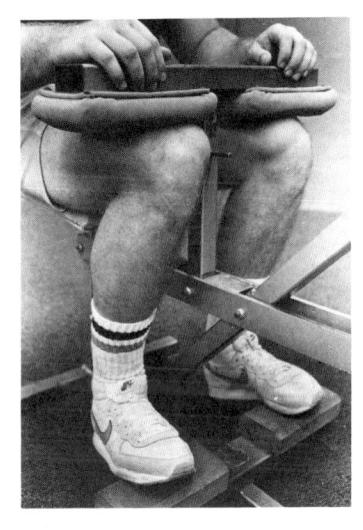

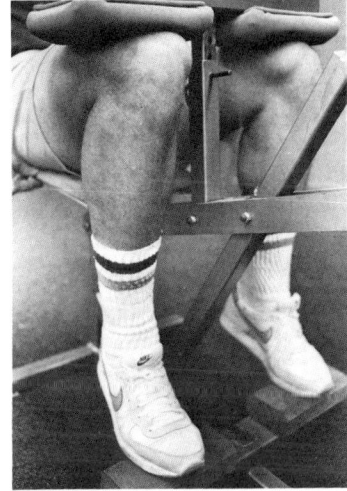

Figure 9-6. Toe raise I

Figure 9-7. Toe raise II

Universal — toe raises
1. Assume sitting position.
2. Place foot on foot pads and adjust height of knee pads for proper fit.
3. Raise weight by lifting heels.

CHEST — BACK — ARMS

Universal parallel dip
(pectorals)
1. Jump to hang support bending knees slightly and crossing legs at ankles. See Fig. 9-8.
2. Slowly lower body until forearms are at a 45 degree angle or greater. See Fig. 9-9.
3. Straighten arms assuming original position.
4. Do not move legs up and down. Force the arms to do all of the work.
5. Negative work may be accomplished by doing just the lowering phase, but this must be done very slowly (5 seconds).

Fig. 9-8. Parallel dip I

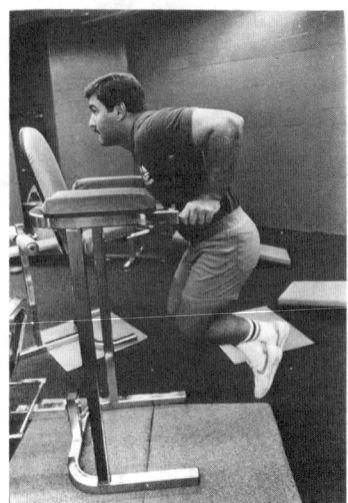

Fig. 9-9. Parallel dip II

Fig. 9-10. Bench press I

Fig. 9-11. Bench press II

Universal — bench press
1. Lie flat on the bench with your head close to the machine.
2. The bend of handles should be above the chest and your feet should be on the floor.
3. Press weight up while exhaling; return weights slowly and under control.

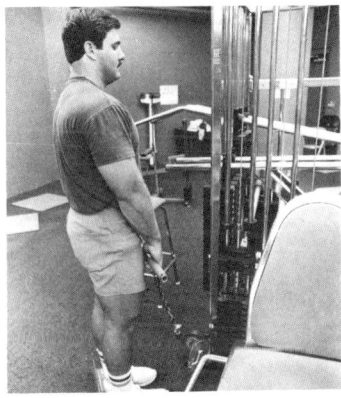

Fig. 9-12. Upright rowing I   **Fig. 9-13.** Upright rowing II

Universal — upright rowing
1. Adjust chain and bar so that bar rests across thighs at arm's length. See Fig. 9-12.
2. Slowly pull bar to chin. See Fig. 9-13.
3. Slowly allow arms to move back to original position.
4. Note: It should take approximately twice the time to lower a weight as it does to raise it.

Universal — seated press
1. Sit facing machine, shoulders almost touching handles. See Fig. 9-14.
2. If possible, place feet inside rungs of bench. This will prevent pushing with your legs.
3. Press upward, trying to keep back flat, and exhaling as the arms move up. Think about blowing the weight up. See Fig. 9-15.

Fig. 9-14. Seated press I   **Fig. 9-15.** Seated press II

Fig. 9-16. Behind neck press I   **Fig. 9-17.** Behind neck press II

Universal — behind neck press
1. Assume a seated position facing the bar.
2. Arms should be fully extended with a wide grip on the bar. See Fig. 9-16.
3. Tilt head forward and pull bar to base of neck. Exhale as the bar comes down, inhale as it goes up. See Fig. 9-17.

Universal — chinning

Fig. 9-18. Chinning

1. Assume a shoulder width grip.
2. Fully extend then pull to chin level.

Note: Moving hands closer together and farther apart will work your arms more completely. Shifting grips to both overhand and underhand also helps. If you have a tendency to swing, touch floor lightly with toes after each descent.

Fig. 9-19. Triceps extension I 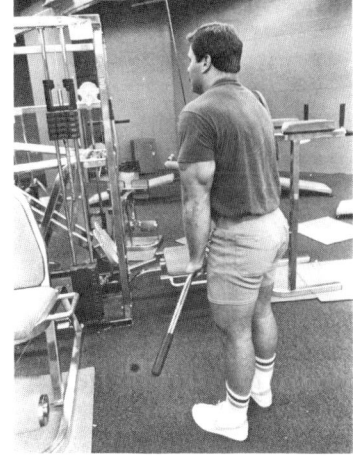   **Fig. 9-20.** Triceps extension II

Universal — triceps extension
1. Assume erect standing position — palms down, hands fairly close together, and elbows in. See Fig. 9-19.
2. Bring bar to shoulder height. Press down and extend arms. Exhale down, inhale up. See Fig. 9-20.
3. Note: Reduce weight if cable touches body.

Universal — shoulder shrug
There are three ways to do the shoulder shrug:
1. Lift straight up and down.
2. Rotate shoulders in a forward circle.
3. Rotate shoulders in a backward circle.

Fig. 9-21. Shoulder shrug I   **Fig. 9-22.** Shoulder shrug II

Fig. 9-23. Arm curl I

Fig. 9-24. Arm curl II

Universal — curls (regular and reverse)
1. Assume palms-up grip — arms extended.
2. Raise bar to near chin level.
3. Slowly lower bar to original position.
4. Repeat process.

Note: To perform the reverse curl turn palms toward floor.

Fig. 9-25. Wrist curl

Universal — wrist roller
1. Regular wrist curl — Place hands on grips, palms down. Bend wrists **away** from you. See Fig. 9-25.
2. Reverse wrist curl — Bend wrists **toward** you.
3. Pronated wrist curl — Place hands on the door knob end and rotate in both directions.

See Chapter Evaluation, Appendix D.

Chapter 10

THE NAUTILUS CONCEPT

By Ellington Darden, Ph.D.
Director of Research
Nautilus Sports/Medical Industries

In 1970, after 20 years of experimentation, Arthur Jones built and sold an exercise machine. It was a pullover machine for the torso muscles. This was the first tool on the market to provide full-range, variable resistance. The resistance was varied by the use of carefully designed spiral pulleys.

As Jones was studying the spiral pulleys, it occurred to him that they resembled a cross section of the chambered nautilus shell. The chambered nautilus is a mollusk which, because of its geometric perfection, has survived at the bottom of the Pacific Ocean for millions of years. It was an ideal symbol for the machines. A year later, the new company in Lake Helen, Florida, became Nautilus Sports/Medical Industries.*

In the last 20 years, Nautilus has developed a unique system of physical conditioning, manufactured and sold thousand of exercise machines, and conducted an enormous amount of exercise-related research. Brief summaries of some of the more important Nautilus findings and descriptions of how to organize a successful Nautilus training program are discussed in this chapter.

---

*For a copy of the latest edition of *The Nautilus Book: An Illustrated Guide to Physical Fitness the Nautilus Way,* send $8.00 to Dr. Darden, P.O. Box 1783, Deland, FL 32720.

Muscular growth

Much confusion exists concerning the complex interaction behind what makes a muscle grow larger and stronger. A simplification of the most up-to-date research reveals that muscular growth is dependent on three factors:

1. There must be growth stimulation within the body itself at the basic cellular level. After puberty this is best accomplished by high-intensity exercise.

2. Stimulated muscles must be permitted to grow. Muscles grow, not during exercise, but during the following 48 hours. The individual must spend sufficient time resting between training sessions.

3. The proper nutrients must be available for the stimulated cells. **But providing large amounts of nutrients in excess of what the body requires does not promote growth of muscle fibers.** The growth machinery within the cell must be turned on. Muscle stimulation and rest must always precede nutrition. If an individual has stimulated muscular growth by high-intensity exercise, his/her muscles will grow from almost any reasonable diet combined with adequate rest.

Stimulation, rest, and **nutrition,** in that order, are the primary requirements for muscular growth.

High-intensity exercise

Muscle stimulation is to a large degree related to the **intensity** of the exercise. The higher the intensity, the better the stimulation. The exercise should be terminated only when no additional repetitions are possible. Intensity and momentary muscular failure are general concepts that must be understood in relation to the time factors involved.

Skeletal muscle growth is produced by working within the anaerobic metabolic processes. The anaerobic metabolic processes are taxed best by intensive exercise that lasts at least 30 seconds, but not more than 70 seconds. Less than 30 seconds of a given exercise does not make sufficient inroads into the muscle's reserve ability. More than 70 seconds of an exercise may involve the aerobic processes, or heart or lungs, to a greater degree than the skeletal muscles.

Empirical evidence seems to reveal that trainees might profit more by counting time rather than counting repetitions. Each set should be continued until momentary muscular failure. That failure should occur between 30 and 70 seconds.

Fast versus slow repetitions

A force plate is a delicate measuring device that can be connected to an oscilloscope. Accurate measurements of force can be recorded by having an individual stand on the plate as he performs an exercise. The difference on the scope between the performance of fast and slow repetitions is dramatic.

Fast repetitions produce peaks and drops on the oscilloscope. These peaks and drops indicate that a 100-pound barbell, for example, can exert from over 500 pounds of force to less than zero. Such erratic force is not only unproductive as far as muscle stimulation is concerned, but is also very dangerous to the joints, muscles, and connective tissues.

Slow, steady repetitions produce a relatively smooth tracing on the scope. This indicates that the resistance is being directed upon the muscle throughout the exercise's range of movement.

The research performed at Nautilus laboratories over the last 20 years proves that **slow repetitions are much more productive than fast repetitions for strength-building purposes.** As a general rule, each repetition should take approximately six seconds to perform — two seconds to lift the weight and four seconds to lower it. The negative or lowering phase of each repetition should be emphasized.

Accentuate the negative

The performance of most strength-training exercises requires the raising and lowering of resistance. When a trainee raises a barbell, dumbbell, weight stack, or his bodyweight, he is moving against gravity and performing positive work. Lowering a weight under control brings gravity into play in another fashion. The lowering portion of an exercise is termed negative work.

In 1972, Arthur Jones, tired of hearing that negative work was of little value in strength training, decided to conduct a study using pure negative work. Assistants lifted every weight for the subjects involved in the study. The subjects, all conditioned athletes, took the resistance in the contracted position and slowly lowered it. This was continued for 8 to 12 slow negative repetitions. Approximately ten exercises per workout were performed in this fashion. The workouts were repeated every other day for six weeks. The results were amazing. All of the athletes improved in muscular strength, size, and condition to a degree that exceeded everyone's expectations.

After eight more years of research and numerous discussions with physiologists all over the world, it appears that the negative phase of a movement is the single most important component in high-intensity exercise. Trainees should do all they can to accentuate the negative.

Relaxation of non-involved muscles

Most trainees are aware of the importance of choosing exercises that isolate, as much as possible, the largest muscle groups. What many may not be aware of, however, is that isolation of a particular muscle is directly related to the ability to relax the non-involved muscles.

Nautilus has found, for example, that if an individual performs leg extensions for the quadriceps muscles, it is to his advantage to relax the upper body. Excessive gripping with the hands involves many muscles of the forearms and upper arms. Moving the torso forward or sideward brings into action the abdominals or obliques. Even tensing the jaws, squinting the eyes, groaning, and yelling during exercise can weaken the neurological input to a given area of the body. The trainee's intention in performing leg extensions is to build muscular size and strength in the quadriceps. Relaxing all other muscles while slowly contracting the quadriceps will help him involve the maximum possible fibers.

Intense stress placed on too many muscles at the same time is not only unproductive, but dangerous. Headaches during the exercise are often a first sign of the trainee's inability to relax non-involved muscles. **An individual can release greater energy to the isolated muscle by learning to relax his other body parts. This in turn allows for more efficient growth stimulation.**

12 rules for nautilus training

1. Perform one set of 4-6 exercises for the lower body and 6-8 exercises for the upper body, and no more than 12 exercises in any workout.
2. Select a resistance on each exercise that allows the performance of between 8-12 repetitions.
3. Continue each exercise until no additional repetitions are possible. When 12 or more repetitions are performed, increase the resistance by approximately 5 percent at the next workout.
4. Work the largest muscles first and move quickly from one exercise to the next. This procedure develops cardiorespiratory endurance.
5. Concentrate on flexibility by slowly stretching during the first three repetitions of each exercise.
6. Accentuate the lowering portion of each repetition.
7. Move slower, never faster, if in doubt about the speed of movement.
8. Do everything possible to isolate and work each large muscle group to exhaustion.
9. Attempt constantly to increase the number of repetitions or the amount of weight, or both. But do not sacrifice form to attempt to produce results.
10. Train no more than three times a week.
11. Keep accurate records — date, resistance, repetitions, and overall training time — of each workout.
12. Vary the workouts often.

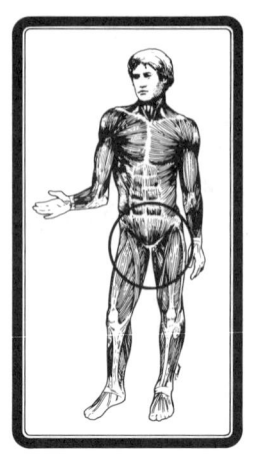

Hips, Waist, Thighs

DUOsymmetric/POLYcontractile HIP & BACK MACHINE

(gluteus maximus, hamstrings, and erector spinea group)
1. Enter machine from front by separating movement arms.
2. Lie on back with both legs over roller pads.
3. Align hip joint with axes of cams.
4. Fasten seat belt and grasp handles lightly. Seat belt should be snug, but not too tight, as back must be arched at completion of movement.
5. Extend both legs and at the same time push back with arms.
6. Keep one leg at full extension, allow other leg to bend and come back as far as possible.
7. Stretch.
8. Push out until it joins other leg at extension.
9. Pause, arch lower back, and contract buttocks. In contracted position, keep legs straight, knees together, and toes pointed.
10. Repeat with other leg.

HIP ABDUCTION-ADDUCTION MACHINE

Hip abduction
(gluteus medius of outer hips)
1. Adjust lever on right side of machine until both movement arms are together.
2. Move thigh pads to the outer position.

Figure 10-1. Hip and back machine — stretched position, left buttocks; contracted position, right buttocks

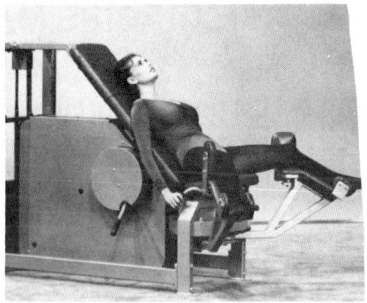

Figure 10-2. Hip abduction-adduction machine

3. Sit in machine and place knees and ankles on movement arms. The outer thighs and knees should be firmly against the resistance pads.
4. Fasten seat belt.
5. Keep head and shoulders against seat back.
6. Spread knees and thighs to widest possible position.
7. Pause.
8. Return to knees-together position and repeat.

Hip adduction
(adductor muscles of inner thighs)
1. Adjust lever on right side of machine for range of movement. The farther the handle is pulled up the greater the range of the machine.
2. Move the thigh pads to the inside position.
3. Sit in machine and place knees and ankles on movement arms in a spread-legged position. The inner thighs and knees should be firmly against the resistance pads.
4. Fasten seat belt.
5. Keep head and shoulders against seat back.
6. Pull knees and thighs smoothly together.
7. Pause in knees-together position.
8. Return slowly to stretched position and repeat.

Important: To better isolate the adductor muscles, keep the feet pointed inward and pull with the thighs, not the lower legs.

MULTI EXERCISE MACHINE
Calf raise
1. Adjust belt comfortably around hips.
2. Place balls of feet on first step and hands on front of carriage.
3. Lock knees and keep locked throughout the movement.
4. Elevate heels as high as possible and try to stand on big toes.
5. Pause.
6. Lower heels slowly.
7. Stretch at bottom by lifting toes.
8. Repeat.

Triceps extension
1. Loop a lightweight towel through weight belt.
2. Grasp one end of towel in each hand. Stand and face away from machine. Arms should be bent with elbows by ears.
3. Adjust grip on towel until weight stack is separated.
4. Straighten arms in a very smooth fashion.
5. Pause.
6. Lower resistance slowly and repeat.

Parallel dip
(Negative only with or without weight belt)
1. Adjust carriage to proper level. It is important to stretch in bottom position.
2. Climb steps.
3. Lock elbows and bend legs.
4. Lower body slowly by bending arms (8-10 seconds).
5. Stretch at bottom position.
6. Climb up and repeat.

Chin-up
(Negative only with or without weight belt)
1. Place cross-bar on forward position.
2. Adjust carriage to proper height. When standing on top step, chin should be barely over bar.
3. Grasp cross-bar with palms up.
4. Climb steps.
5. Place chin over bar, elbows by sides, and legs bent.

Figure 10-3. Multi exercise machine side bend

Figure 10-4. Multi exercise machine — toe rise with bend

6. Lower body slowly (8-10 seconds).
7. Stretch at bottom position.
8. Climb up and repeat.

Important: Movement can also be done in a behind neck fashion by using parallel grip.

Wrist curl

1. Sit in front of machine, using small bench or chair, with toes under first step.
2. Attach small bar directly to movement arm.
3. Grasp handles in a palms-up fashion. (Palms-down grip should also be used.)
4. Place forearms firmly against thighs.
5. Curl small bar upward.
6. Pause.
7. Lower resistance slowly and repeat.

Important: Do not move forearms. Only hands should move. Keep knees close together. Avoid jerky movements.

Other movements

Biceps curl,
Shoulder shrug,
Bent-over row,
Hanging leg raise, side bend.

Figure 10-5
Abdominal machine

ABDOMINAL MACHINE

(rectus abdominis)
1. Sit in machine.
2. Locate axis of rotation on right side.
3. Adjust seat so axis of rotation is at same level as lower part of sternum or breastbone.
4. Place ankles behind roller pads.
5. Spread knees and sit erect.
6. Grasp handles.
7. Keep shoulders and head firmly against seat back.
8. Shorten the distance between rib cage and navel by contracting abdominals only. Do not pull with latissimus or triceps muscles.
9. Keep legs relaxed as seat bottom is elevated.
10. Pause in contracted position.
11. Return slowly to starting position and repeat.

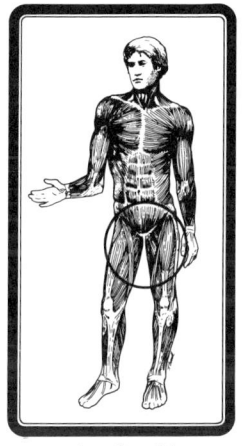

Buttocks, Quadriceps, Hamstrings

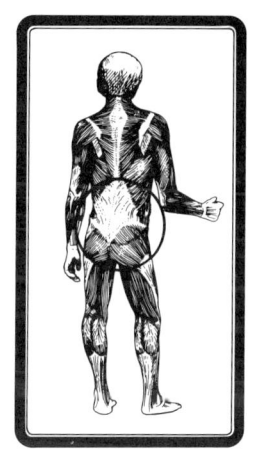

Lower back and Buttocks

COMPOUND LEG MACHINE

Leg extension
(frontal thighs or quadriceps)
1. Place feet behind roller pads, with knees snug against seat.
2. Adjust seat back to comfortable position.
3. Keep head and shoulders against seat back.
4. Straighten both legs smoothly.
5. Pause.
6. Lower resistance slowly and repeat.
7. Move quickly to leg press after final repetition.

Figure 10-6. Compound leg machine — leg extension, finished position

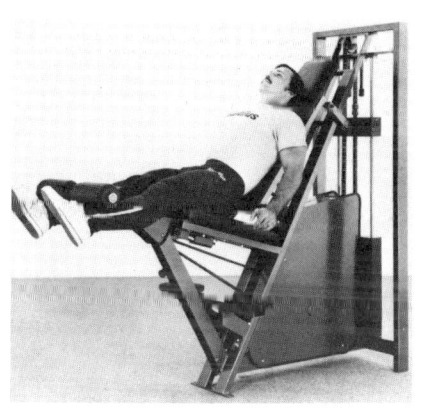

Figure 10-7. Compound leg machine — leg extension, beginning position

Figure 10-8. Compound leg machine
— leg press, finishing position

Leg press
(quadriceps, hamstrings, and gluteus maximus)
1. Sit erect and pull seat back forward.
2. Flip down foot pads.
3. Place both feet on pads with toes pointed slightly inward.
4. Straighten both legs in a controlled manner.
5. Return to stretched position and repeat.

   Important: Avoid tightly gripping handles and do not grit teeth or tense neck or face muscles during either movement.

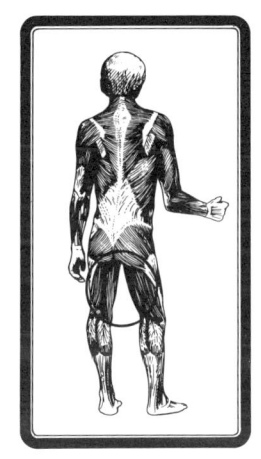

Hamstrings

LEG CURL MACHINE

(hamstrings)
1. Lie face down on machine.
2. Place feet under roller pads with knees just over edge of bench.
3. Grasp handles to keep body from moving.
4. Curl legs and try to touch heels to buttocks.
5. Lift buttocks to increase range of movement.
6. Pause at point of full contraction.
7. Lower resistance slowly and repeat.

   Important: Top of foot should be flexed toward knee throughout movement.

Figure 10-9. Leg curl machine — full hamstring contraction

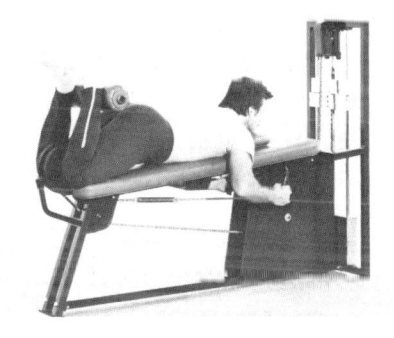

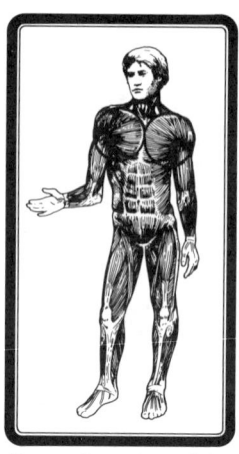

Pectoralis majors of the
chest and deltoids
of shoulders

DOUBLE CHEST MACHINE

Arm cross
(pectoralis majors of the chest and deltoids of shoulders)
1. Adjust seat until shoulders, when elbows are together, are directly under axes of overhead cams.
2. Fasten seat belt.
3. Place forearms behind and firmly against movement arm pads.
4. Grasp handles lightly, thumbs should be around handle, and keep head against seat back.
5. Push with forearms and try to touch elbows together in front of chest. (Movement can also be done one arm at a time in an alternate fashion.)
6. Pause.
7. Lower resistance slowly and repeat. After final repetition, immediately do decline press.

Decline press
(chest, shoulders, and triceps of arms)
1. Use foot pedal to raise handles into starting position.
2. Grasp handles with parallel grip.
3. Keep head back and torso erect.
4. Press bars forward in controlled fashion.
5. Lower resistance slowly keeping elbows wide.
6. Stretch in bottom position and repeat pressing movement.

Figure 10-10. Double chest machine — arm cross, beginning position

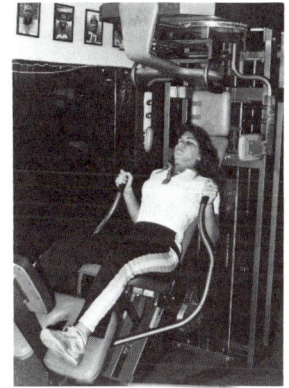

Figure 10-11. Double chest machine — decline press

DOUBLE SHOULDER MACHINE

Lateral raise
(deltoid muscles of shoulders)
1. Adjust seat so shoulder joints are in line with axes of cams.
2. Position thighs on seat, cross ankles, and fasten seat belt.
3. Pull handles back until knuckles touch pads.
4. Lead with elbows and raise both arms until parallel with floor.
5. Pause.
6. Lower resistance slowly and repeat. After final repetition, immediately do overhead press.

   Important: Keep knuckles against pads and elbows high at all times.

Figure 10-12. Double shoulder machine — lateral raise, contracted position

Overhead press
(deltoids and triceps)
1. Raise seat quickly for greater range of movement.
2. Grasp handles above shoulders.
3. Press handles overhead while being careful not to arch back.
4. Lower resistance slowly keeping elbows wide, and repeat.

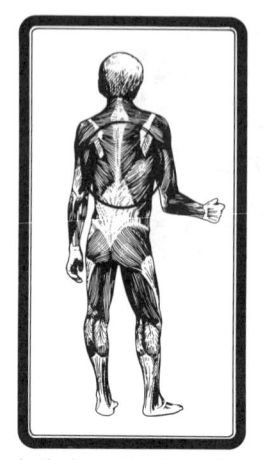

Latissimus dorsi muscles of the back and other torso muscles, including abdominals

Figure 10-13. Pullover machine, stretched position

PULLOVER MACHINE (plateloading)
(latissimus dorsi of the back and other torso muscles)
1. Adjust seat so shoulder joints are in line with axes of cams.
2. Assume erect position and fasten seat belt tightly.
3. Leg press foot pedal until elbow pads are about chin level.
4. Place elbows on pads. Hands should be open and resting on curved portion of bar.
5. Remove legs from pedal and slowly rotate elbows as far back as possible.
6. Stretch.
7. Rotate elbows down until bar touches midsection.
8. Pause.
9. Return slowly to stretched position and repeat.

Important: Look straight ahead during movement. Do not move head or torso. Do not grip tightly with hands.

Figure 10-14. Behind neck/torso arm machine — pulldown

Figure 10-15. Behind neck machine, finished position

COMBINATION BEHIND NECK/TORSO ARM MACHINE

Behind neck
(latissimus dorsi of the back)
1. Adjust seat so shoulder joints are in line with axes of cams.
2. Fasten seat belt.
3. Place back of upper arms (triceps area) between padded movement arms.
4. Cross forearms behind neck.
5. Move both arms downward until perpendicular to floor.
6. Pause.
7. Return slowly to crossed-arm position behind neck and repeat. After final repetition, immediately do behind neck pulldown.

   Important: Be careful not to bring arms or hands to front of body.

Behind neck pulldown
(latissimus dorsi of the back and biceps of upper arms)
1. Lean forward and grasp overhead bar with parallel grip.
2. Pull bar behind neck, keeping elbows back.
3. Pause.
4. Return slowly to starting position and repeat.

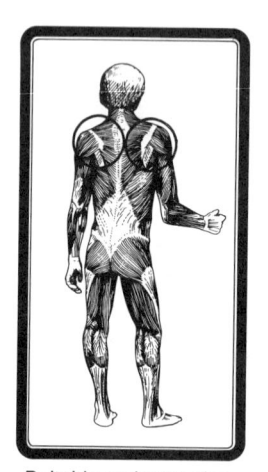

Deltoids and trapezius

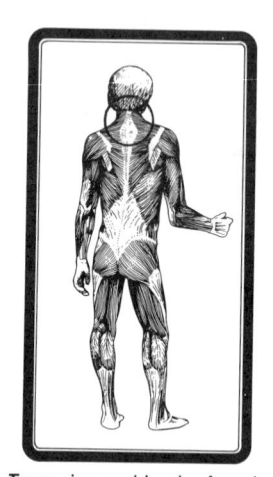

Trapezius and back of neck

Figure 10-16. Rowing machine, extended postion

ROWING MACHINE

(deltoids and trapezius)
1. Sit with back toward weight stack.
2. Place arms between pads and cross arms.
3. Bend arms in rowing fashion as far back as possible.
4. Pause.
5. Return slowly to starting position and repeat.

   Important: Keep arms parallel to floor at all times.

NECK & SHOULDER MACHINE

(trapezius and back of neck)
1. Place forearms between pads while seated.
2. Keep palms open and back of hands pressed against bottom pads.
3. Straighten torso until weight stack is lifted. Seat may be raised with elevation pads.
4. Shrug shoulders smoothly as high as possible.
5. Pause.
6. Return slowly to stretched position and repeat.

Important: Keep elbows by sides when shrugging. Do not lean back or try to stand while doing the movement. Do not rest weights on stack during movement.

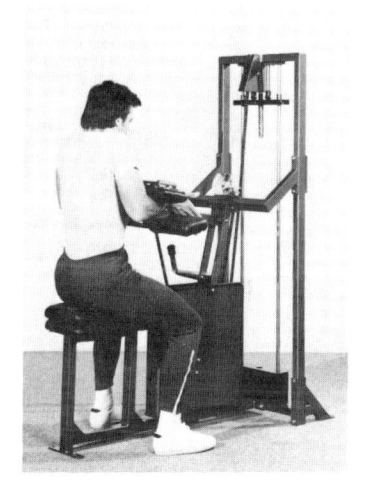

Figure 10-17.
Neck and shoulder machine — shoulder shrug

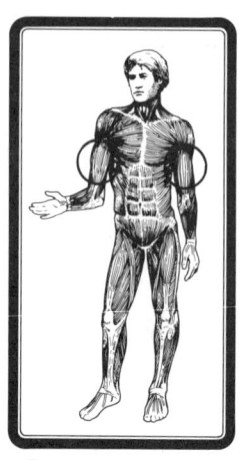

Biceps of upper arms

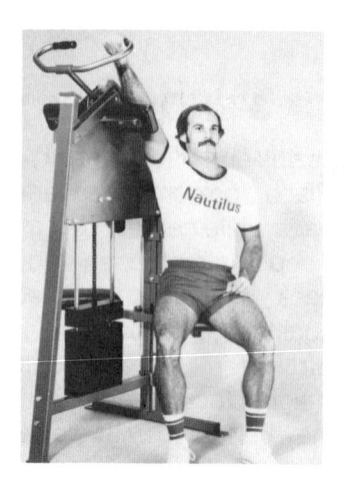

Figure 10-18. Compound curl machine, beginning position

COMPOUND POSITION CURL MACHINE
(biceps of the upper arm)
1. Be seated on the left side of the machine to work the right biceps.
2. Adjust the seat so the elbow is in line with the axis of the cam.
3. Grasp the handle lightly with an underhand grip.
4. Curl the handle behind the neck.
5. Pause.
6. Lower the movement arm slowly and repeat.
7. Reverse the procedure for working the left biceps on the right side of the machine.

MULTI BICEPS MACHINE
(biceps of upper arms)
1. Place elbows on pad and in line with the axes of cams.
2. Adjust seat so shoulders are slightly lower than elbows. Machine can be used in at least eight different ways.

Two arms normal
1. Curl both arms to the contracted position.
2. Pause.
3. Lower slowly to the stretched position and repeat.

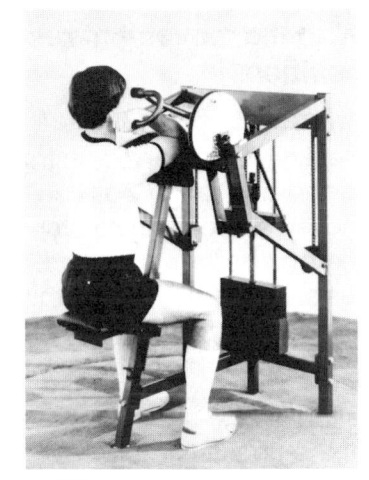

Figure 10-19
Multi-biceps machine

Two arms alternate
1. Do a complete repetition with one arm.
2. Do another complete repetition with the opposite arm.
3. Alternate back and forth until momentary muscular exhaustion.

Two arms duo-poly
1. Bring both arms to the contracted position.
2. Holding one arm in the contracted position, lower the resistance with the opposite arm, and curl the movement arm back to the contracted position.
3. Repeat with the other arm.

   Remember: one arm must always be in the contracted position while the other arm is moving.

One arm normal
1. Work one arm to exhaustion, usually the non-dominant arm first.
2. Work the other arm to exhaustion.

   Note: a trainee will be able to handle slightly more resistance with one arm than with two.

One arm negative emphasized
1. Use the opposite arm for assistance in curling a heavier-than-normal weight.
2. Lower slowly the resistance arm (8-10 seconds) with one arm.
3. Continue in this fashion until the biceps is unable to control the downward movement.
4. Repeat the procedure with the other arm.

With the movement restraining stop in the center position

Infimetric
Remove the selector pin from the weight stack. Curl both arms to the mid-range position, or until contact is made with the movement restraining stop. In order for one arm to straighten, the other arm must bend. The trainee can vary the force by resisting more or less with the unbending arm. The movement should be smooth and steady with no dropping of the weight.

Isometric
Same procedure as infimetric, except do not permit movement of the unbending arm. Since a person is 40% stronger negatively than positively, the negative arm is always able to prevent movement in the positive arm. It is possible therefore to provide an isometric or static contraction at any point along the range of movement of the machine.

Akinetic
The primary difference between infimetric and akinetic is in infimetric the selector pin is not used, while in akinetic a predetermined amount of resistance is used. With infimetric training, it is very difficult to estimate the amount of force that is being exerted during the movement. With akinetic training, however, a medium resistance is selected and although a trainee can exert more force, any time he exerts less force, the weight stack drops noticeably.

MULTI TRICEPS MACHINE
(triceps of upper arms)
1. Adjust seat so shoulders are slightly lower than elbows.
2. Place sides of hands on movement arms and elbows on pad and in line with the axes of cams. Machine can be used in at least eight different ways.

Two-arms normal
1. Straighten arms to the contracted position.
2. Pause.
3. Lower slowly to the stretched position and repeat.

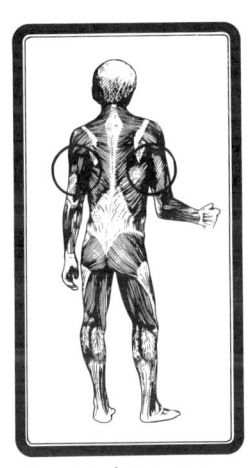

Triceps of upper arms

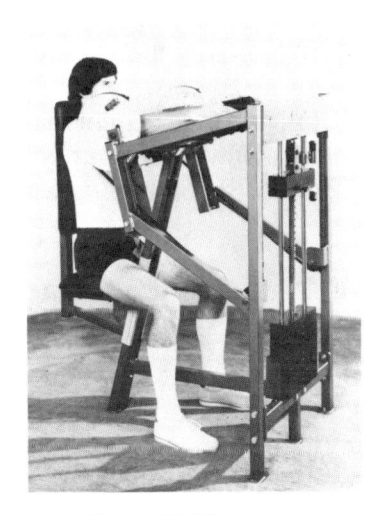

Figure 10-20
Multi-triceps machine

Two arms alternate
1. Do a complete repetition with one arm.
2. Do another complete repetition with the opposite arm.
3. Alternate back and forth until momentary muscular exhaustion.

Two arms duo-poly
1. Straighten both arms to the contracted position.
2. Holding one arm in the contracted position, lower the resistance with the opposite arm, and return to the contracted position.
3. Repeat with the other arm.

One arm normal
1. Work one arm to exhaustion, usually the non-dominant arm first.
2. Work the other arm to exhaustion.

    Note: a trainee will be able to handle slightly more resistance with one arm than with two.

One arm negative-emphasized
1. Use the opposite arm for assistance in lifting a heavier-than-normal weight.
2. Lower slowly the resistance arm (8-10 seconds) with one arm.
3. Continue in this fashion until the triceps is unable to control the downward movement.
4. Repeat the procedure with the other arm.

With the movement restraining stop in the center position

Infimetric
Remove the selector pin from the weight stack. Extend both arms to the mid-range position, or until contact is made with the movement restraining stop. In order for one arm to straighten, the other arm must bend. The trainee can vary the force by resisting more or less with the bending arm. The movement should be smooth and steady with no dropping of the weight.

Isometric
Same procedure as infimetric, except do not permit movement of the bending arm. Since a person is 40% stronger negatively than positively, the negative arm is always able to prevent movement in the positive arm. It is possible therefore to provide an isometric or static contraction at any point along the range of movement of the machine.

Akinetic
The primary difference between infimetric and akinetic is in infimetric the selector pin is not used, while in akinetic a predetermined amount of resistance is used. With infimetric training, it is very difficult to estimate the amount of force that is being exerted during the movement. With akinetic training, however, a medium resistance is selected and although a trainee can exert more force, any time he exerts less force, the weight stack drops noticeably.

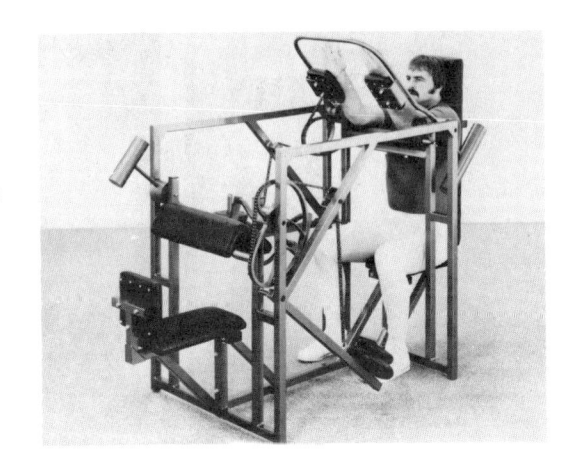

Figure 10-21
Biceps/triceps machine

BICEPS/TRICEPS MACHINE (plateloading)

Biceps curl
(biceps of upper arms)
1. Enter machine from left side.
2. Place elbows on pad and in line with axis of cam.
3. Grasp bar with hands together and palms up.
4. Curl bar smoothly until it reaches neck.
5. Pause.
6. Return slowly to stretched position and repeat.

   Important: Lean back at full extension to insure stretching.

Triceps extension
(triceps of upper arms)
1. Adjust seated position, with pads if necessary, until shoulders are on same level as elbows.
2. Place elbows in line with axis of cam and hands with thumbs up on pads.
3. Straighten arms smoothly.
4. Pause.
5. Return slowly to stretched position and repeat.

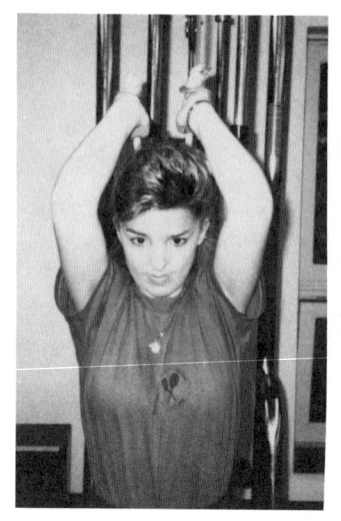

Figure 10-22. All-purpose machine — triceps extension, beginning position

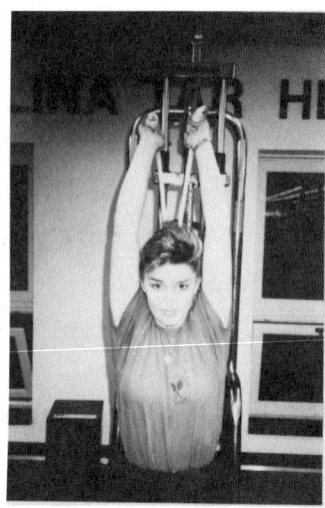

Figure 10-23. All-purpose machine — triceps extension, ending position

ALL PURPOSE MACHINE
Triceps extension
1. Loop a lightweight towel through weight belt.
2. Grasp one end of towel in each hand. Stand and face away from machine.
3. Arms should now be bent with elbows by ears.
4. Adjust grip on towel until weight stack is separated.
5. Straighten arms in a very smooth fashion.
6. Pause.
7. Slowly lower resistance and repeat.

4/WAY NECK MACHINE
Anterior flexion
(front of neck)
1. Face machine.
2. Adjust seat so nose is in center of pads.
3. Stabilize torso by lightly grasping handles.
4. Move head smoothly toward chest.
5. Pause.
6. Return slowly to stretched position and repeat.

   Important: Do not use torso or legs to assist neck. Good form is a must.

Rotation of neck and head to right and left

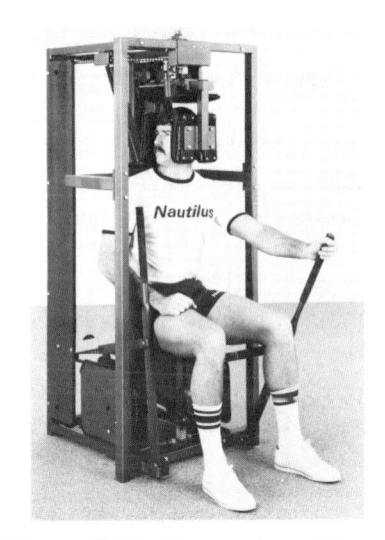

Figure 10-24. 4/way neck machine

Posterior extension
(back of neck)
1. Turn body in machine until back of head contacts center of pads.
2. Stabilize torso by lightly grasping handles.
3. Extend head as far back as possible.
4. Pause.
5. Return slowly to stretched position and repeat.

Lateral contraction
(side of neck)
1. Turn body in machine until left ear is in center of pads.
2. Stabilize torso by lightly grasping handles.
3. Move head toward left shoulder.
4. Pause.
5. Keep shoulders square.
6. Return slowly to stretched position and repeat.
7. Reverse procedure for right side.

A BEGINNING NAUTILUS PROGRAM

Nautilus Sports/Medical Industries manufactures over 30 different exercise machines. Full sets of these machines are now available all over the United States in fitness centers, in many colleges and universities, in high schools, and in the training rooms of many professional sports teams.

A beginning trainee should perform the following routine daily for a period of five days in a row. One set of 8-12 repetitions should be done on each exercise.

1. Hip and back
2. Compound leg, leg extension
3. Compound leg, leg press
4. Leg curl
5. Double shoulder, lateral raise
6. Double shoulder, overhead press
7. Pullover
8. Double chest, arm cross
9. Double chest, decline press
10. Biceps/triceps, curl
11. Biceps/triceps, extension

During the first workout, the selection of the weight to use will be trial and error. The listing below offers guidelines for the appropriate weight. Women will have to start with less resistance on most machines.

```
Hip & back (Duo-Poly) . . . . . . . . . . . . . . . . .60 pounds
Compound leg, leg extension . . . . . . . . . . .60 pounds
Compound leg, leg press. . . . . . . . . . . . . . .80 pounds
Leg curl . . . . . . . . . . . . . . . . . . . . . . . . . . . . .40 pounds
Double shoulder, lateral raise . . . . . . . . . . .40 pounds
Double shoulder, overhead press . . . . . . . .40 pounds
Pullover . . . . . . . . . . . . . . . . . . . . . . . . . . . . .50 pounds
Double chest, arm cross . . . . . . . . . . . . . . .40 pounds
Double chest, decline press . . . . . . . . . . . .60 pounds
Biceps/triceps (plateloading), curl . . . . . . . .25 pounds
Biceps/triceps (plateloading), extension . . .25 pounds
```

The top plate on all Nautilus machines with self-contained weight stacks weighs 10 pounds. The selector rod weighs 10 pounds also. Thus, the lightest weight available is 20 pounds. Each plate weighs 10 pounds. To put on 50 pounds on the pullover machine, the individual would count the top plate and selector rod as 20 and place the selector pin in the third hole from the top. Substitutions can be made if the listed Nautilus machines are not available.

If the trainee is unable to perform at least 8 repetitions with the suggested weight, the weight is too heavy; more than 12, and the weight is too light. By the end of the first week of training, the individual should know the correct resistance for each machine.

Some muscular soreness can be expected during the first week of training. But by training for five days in a row, most athletes will avoid severe muscular soreness. After the first five workouts, a 72-hour rest should be permitted before resuming training on a regular basis. Thus, the individual might train Monday through Friday during the first week, then skip Saturday and Sunday, and resume training on Monday.

Starting on Monday of the second week and every week thereafter, the trainee should work out only three times, or every other day with a 72-hour rest after every three sessions.

In all exercises, the individual should continue to the point at which another repetition in good form is impossible. He should not, however, stop simply because 12 repetitions have been reached.

The above routine should be continued for at least four weeks and perhaps as much as twelve weeks. But in any case it should be followed until such time as the athlete is gaining rapidly in strength.

The program should not be changed until the individual is capable of performing at least 12 repetitions with the following resistance on these Nautilus machines:

```
Hip and back . . . . . . . . . . . . . . . . . . . . . . . . .90 pounds
Leg extension . . . . . . . . . . . . . . . . . . . . . . . .90 pounds
Leg press . . . . . . . . . . . . . . . . . . . . . . . . . .120 pounds
Pullover . . . . . . . . . . . . . . . . . . . . . . . . . . . .90 pounds
Decline press . . . . . . . . . . . . . . . . . . . . . . .100 pounds
Biceps curl . . . . . . . . . . . . . . . . . . . . . . . . . .40 pounds
Triceps extension . . . . . . . . . . . . . . . . . . . . .40 pounds
```

Some trainees will reach the above strength levels very quickly; others will take longer. But advanced training should not be undertaken at strength levels much, if any, below those listed. Once a basic level of strength is established, the individual is ready to advance.

ADVANCED NAUTILUS TRAINING

The athlete should not make the mistake of thinking that the stronger he becomes, the more exercises he can perform. This is not the case! Never should an athlete perform over 12 exercises, one set of each, in any one workout. In many cases, the number must be reduced to 10, or even 8. Nautilus training should not be performed more than three times a week, and even this number may have to be reduced. The stronger the individual becomes, the less exercise he needs.

At the advanced level, variety can be introduced into the trainee's Nautilus workouts. The individual is now ready to use other Nautilus machines such as the Multi-Exercise, 4-Way Neck, and Hip Abduction-Adduction, and other styles of training such as negative-only and negative-accentuated. Negative training was briefly discussed earlier; but generally speaking, when an athlete lifts a weight, he is performing positive work. When he lowers a weight, he is performing negative work.

Since an individual is approximately 40 percent stronger lowering a weight than he/she is raising it, concentrating on the lowering part of the exercise produces faster results. This can be accomplished in several different ways: (1) by having two assistants raise a heavier weight than he/she normally uses, and he/she then lowers it slowly (negative only), (2) by using the legs to do the positive part of the movement and then slowly lowering the resistance with the arms or upper body. Nautilus Omni machines have special foot pedal/leg press attachments for this, or the steps of the Multi-Exercise machine can be used in this fashion for chins and dips. Negative-accentuated training can be performed by lifting the movement arm with both limbs and lowering it slowly with only one.

The following Nautilus machines or exercises can be performed in a negative-only fashion.

Leg curl	4-Way neck
Leg press	Rotary neck
Pullover	Chin
Lateral raise	Dip
Overhead press	Omni biceps
Decline press	Omni triceps
Neck and shoulder	

Negative-accentuated exercise can be performed with these machines:

- Leg extension
- Leg press
- Pullover
- Overhead press
- Decline press
- Biceps/triceps (plateloading)
- Omni biceps
- Omni triceps
- Calf raise

All of the following Nautilus routines have been used successfully by athletes. An individual can alternate any of them with his basic workout, or he can design his own routine, keeping in mind the 12 rules.

Alternate nautilus routines

1
1. Hip abduction-adduction
2. Leg curl
3. Leg extension
4. Leg press
5. Calf raise on multi exercise
6. Behind neck
7. Behind neck pulldown
8. Triceps extension with towel on multi-exercise
9. Side bend on multi-exercise
10. 4-Way neck
11. Neck and shoulder
12. Wrist curl

2
1. Overhead press
2. Chin on multi-exercise
3. Decline press
4. Behind neck pulldown
5. Dip on multi-exercise
6. Pullover
7. Rotary torso
8. Lateral raise
9. Leg extension
10. Leg press
11. Hip and back
12. Abdominal

3
1. Leg extension (NA)
2. Leg press (NA)
3. Leg curl (NA)
4. Lateral raise (NO)
5. Overhead press (NO)
6. Pullover (NO)
7. Chin (NO)
8. Dip (NO)
9. Neck and shoulder (NO)
10. Rotary neck (NO)

4
1. Leg press (NO)
2. Leg extension
3. Leg curl (NO)
4. Calf raise (NA)
5. Arm cross
6. Decline press (NO)
7. Duo-Poly pullover
8. Overhead press (NA)
9. Rowing torso
10. Omni triceps (NO)
11. Omni biceps (NO)

(NO) = Negative only
(NA) = Negative accentuated

See Chapter Evaluation, Appendix D.

Chapter 11
SPECIAL WEIGHT TRAINING PROGRAMS

One of the most controversial questions in the field of athletic conditioning is the relationship between increases in strength and improved performance.

Most scientists do not question the fact that strength is a highly desirable ingredient for success in any sport. However, what troubles most researchers is that once a certain level of strength is obtained, acquisition of additional strength does not produce a corresponding increase in performance.

The optimal levels of strength for various sports have not been determined at this time. Therefore, most athletes and coaches take the position that they will profit by increasing what they have. Since playing a sport only produces minimal levels of strength, it becomes necessary for sports participants to engage in specially designed exercises if they are to increase their strength to higher levels.

The following weight training programs have been developed to assist you in acquiring additional strength for those muscles most used in your particular sport. The first two programs are sample Nautilus and Free Weight — Universal programs. At the close of this chapter you will find additional Weight Training Record Sheets which may be easily removed for your convenience.

SPECIAL WEIGHT TRAINING PROGRAMS

Archery	Jogging
Badminton	Lacrosse
Baseball	Martial arts
Basketball	Muscle toning (general)
Canoeing	Skiing
Chest development	Soccer
Fencing	Swimming
Football	Tennis
Golf	Track
Gymnastics	Volleyball
Hiking	Weight gain
Hip reduction	Weight loss
Hip and thigh	Wrestling
Hockey	

NAME SAMPLE

Exercises: NAUTILUS

MONDAY	Wt. 1 Reps.	Wt. 2 Reps.	Wt. 3 Reps.	Wt. 4 Reps.	Wt. 5 Reps.
Chest Upper	8-12	110 10			
Chest Press	8-12	110 11			
Shoulder Fly	8-12	120 9			
Shoulder Press	8-12	90 10			
Pullover	8-12	120 12			
Pulldown	8-12	70 12			
Multi Ex. Dips	8-12	20 9			
Multi Ex. Chins	8-12	20 10			
Compound Leg Ext.	12-15	120 14			
Compound Leg Press	12-15	150 12			
Leg Curl	12-15	00 15			
Ab-Adductor	12	60 12			

WEDNESDAY

Repeat Exercises	8-12	110 12			
	8-12	110 12			
	8-12	120 12			
	8-12	90 12			
	8-12	130 10			
	8-12	80 11			
	8-12	20 12			
	8-12	20 12			
	12-15	120 15			
	12-15	150 15			
	12-15	70 14			
	12	70 10			

FRIDAY

Repeat Exercises	8-12	120 9			
	8-12	120 10			
	8-12	130 10			
	8-12	100 9			
	8-12	130 12			
	8-12	80 12			
	8-12	30 10			
	8-12	30 10			
	12-15	130 12			
	12-15	160 13			
	12-15	80 12			
	12	70 12			

NAME __SAMPLE__

FREE WEIGHT & UNIVERSAL

3 Days Per Week

EXERCISES:	Date: Reps:	10-1	10-3	10-5	10-8	10-10
Bench	8	135-7	135-8	145-7	145-8	155-7
	6	145-5	145-6	155-5	155-6	165-5
	4	155-3	155-4	165-3	165-4	175-3
	2	165-1	165-2	175-1	175-2	185-1
	1	175-0	175-1	185-0	185-1	195-0
Dumbbell inclines	12	40-10	40-12	50-10	50-12	60-10
		20-20	20-20	25-25	25-25	30-30
Dumbbell lateral raises	12	40-10	40-12	50-10	50-12	60-10
		20-20	20-20	25-25	25-25	30-30
Sitting military	12	85-10	85-12	95-10	95-12	105-10
	8	95-6	95-8	105-6	105-8	115-6
Lat pulldown	12	120-10	120-12	130-10	130-12	140-10
	8	130-8	140-6	140-8	150-6	150-8
Chins	Max	10	11	12	13	14
Dips	Max	20	21	22	20	21
Squats	8	225-7	225-8	235-6	235-8	245-6
	6	235-5	235-6	245-5	245-6	255-5
	4	245-3	245-4	255-3	255-4	265-3
Universal leg ext.	15	100-14	100-15	110-12	110-13	110-15
Universal leg press	15	200-13	200-14	200-15	210-12	210-14
Universal leg curl	15	60-14	60-15	70-12	70-14	70-15
Toe raises	12	70-10	70-12	80-11	80-12	90-10
	12	70-10	70-12	80-11	80-12	90-10
	12	70-10	70-12	80-11	80-12	90-10
Situps	25					
	25					
	25					

NAME _____

Exercises: ARCHERY - Free Weight & Universal — 3 Days Per Week

Exercise	Wt. 1 Reps.	Wt. 2 Reps.	Wt. 3 Reps.	Wt. 4 Reps.	Wt. 5 Reps.
Dumbbell Lateral Raises	12				
High Pulls	12				
Triceps Extension	12				
Biceps Curl	12				
French Curls	12				
Wrist Curls	12				
Forearm Curls	12				

NAME _____

Exercises: ARCHERY - Nautilus   3 Days Per Week

Exercise	Wt. 1 Reps.	Wt. 2 Reps.	Wt. 3 Reps.	Wt. 4 Reps.	Wt. 5 Reps.
Nautilus Double Shoulder	8				
Nautilus Shrug Machine	12				
Nautilus Triceps Machine	8				
Nautilus Biceps Machine	8				
Multi Ex. Forearms Curl	12				
Wrist Curls	12				
Paper Crunches	12				

NAME _____

Exercises: BADMINTON - Nautilus

	Wt. 1 Reps.	Wt. 2 Reps.	Wt. 3 Reps.	Wt. 4 Reps.	Wt. 5 Reps.
Standing Lat Pull	12-8				
Nautilus Pullover	12-8				
Nautilus Chest Fly	12				
Nautilus Shoulder Fly	12				
Nautilus Leg Press	12				
Nautilus Leg Curl	12				
Nautilus Leg Extension	12				

NAME _____

Exercises: BASEBALL IN SEASON

MONDAY	Wt. 1 Reps.	Wt. 2 Reps.	Wt. 3 Reps.	Wt. 4 Reps.	Wt. 5 Reps.
Incline Bench	8	6	4		
High Lat Pull	10	10			
N. Shoulder Press	10	10			
Tricep Pushdown	10	10			
E-Z Bicep Curl	8	8			
N. Leg Press	10	10			
Ab-Adductor	15				
N. Leg Curl	10	8	6		
Ball Throw - 25					
Wrist Curls	15	15			

THURSDAY

Bench Press	8	6	4		
Close Grip Lat	12	8			
DB Lateral Raise	12	8			
E-Z Tricep Press	12	8			
Str. Bar Bicep	12	8			
Leverage Leg Press	10	10			
Hip Flexer	15				
N. Leg Curl	15	10			
Ball Throw - 25					
Wrist Curls	15	15			

NAME _____

Exercises: BASEBALL OFF SEASON

MONDAY

Exercise	Wt.1	Reps.	Wt.2	Reps.	Wt.3	Reps.	Wt.4	Reps.	Wt.5	Reps.
Bench Press		8		6		6				
E-Z Pullover		8		8						
Close Grip Lat		12		8						
DB Lateral Raise		12		8						
Upright Row/Shrugs		8		8						
E-Z Tricep Press		8		8						
Str. Bar Bicep		12		8						
Leverage Leg Press		12		8						
Lunges		12								
N. Leg Curl		15		10						
Ball Throw - 25										
Wrist Curls		15		15						

WEDNESDAY

Exercise	Wt.1	Reps.	Wt.2	Reps.	Wt.3	Reps.	Wt.4	Reps.	Wt.5	Reps.
Incline Bench		8		6		6				
High Lat Pull		10		8						
Chin Ups		15								
N. Shoulder Press		12		8						
Tricep Pushdown		8		8						
E-Z Bicep Curl		12		8						
Manual Bicep Curl		10								
Back Squat		10		10						
Hip Flexer		15								
N. Leg Curl		15		10						
Ball Throw - 25										
Wrist Curls		15		15						

FRIDAY

Exercise	Wt.1	Reps.	Wt.2	Reps.	Wt.3	Reps.	Wt.4	Reps.	Wt.5	Reps.
Bench Press		8		6		6				
E-Z Pullover		12		8						
Close Grip Lat		10		8						
DB Lateral Raise		10		8						
Upright Row/Shrugs		10		8						
E-Z Tricep Press		12		8						
Str. Bar Bicep		10		10						
N. Leg Press		12		8						
Ab-Adductor		15								
N. Leg Curl		15		10						
Ball Throw - 25										
Wrist Curls		15		15						

NAME _____

Exercises: BASKETBALL

MONDAY

Exercise	1 Wt./Reps	2 Wt./Reps	3 Wt./Reps	4 Wt./Reps	5 Wt./Reps
N. Chest Press	12	8			
Chin-Ups	12				
N. Shoulder Press	12	8			
Weighted Dips	10	10			
Manual Bicep	10				
N. Leg Press	12	8			
Hip Flexer	15				
N. Leg Curl	10	10			
Weighted Sit-Ups	15				

WEDNESDAY

Exercise	1	2	3	4	5
Bench Press	12	8			
High Lat Pull	12				
Military Press	12	8			
Tricep Pushdown	12	8			
E-Z Bicep Curl	10	10			
Leg Extension	10	10			
Lunges	12				
N. Leg Curl	10	10			
Crunch Machine	15	15			

FRIDAY

Exercise	1	2	3	4	5
Incline Bench	12	8			
Close Grip Lat	12				
N. Shoulder Fly	8	8			
Weighted Dips	10	10			
Manual Bicep	10				
N. Leg Press	12	8			
Ab-Adductor	15				
N. Leg Curl	10	10			
Weighted Sit-Ups	15				

NAME _____

Exercises: CANOEING - Free Weight & Universal										
	Wt.	1 Reps.	Wt.	2 Reps.	Wt.	3 Reps.	Wt.	4 Reps.	Wt.	5 Reps.
Bench		8		8		8		6		6
Bent-Over Rowing		12								
Chin-Up		12								
Dips		12								
Dumbbell Lateral Raises		12								
Sitting Military		12								
Wrist Curls		12								
Leg Ext. - Universal		15								
Leg Press - Universal		15								
Leg Curls - Universal		15								

NAME _____

Exercises: CANOEING - Nautilus

	Wt. 1 Reps.	Wt. 2 Reps.	Wt. 3 Reps.	Wt. 4 Reps.	Wt. 5 Reps.
Leg Press	15				
Leg Curl	15				
Leg Extension	15				
Hip & Back	15				
Shoulder Press	12				
Chin-Up-Multiex	12				
Chest Press	12				
Behind Neck Pulldown	12				
Dips-Multiex	12				
Pullover	12				
Triceps Extension	12				
Biceps/Curl	12				

NAME _____

Exercises: CHEST DEVELOPMENT - Free Weight & Universal												
	Wt.	**1** Reps	Wt.	**2** Reps	Wt.	**3** Reps	Wt.	**4** Reps	Wt.	**5** Reps	Wt.	**6** Reps
Bench Press		8		6		6		4		4		
Incline Bench		8		6		4						
Dumbbell Chest Flys		12		8								
Dumbbell Chest Press		12		8								
Weighted Dips		12		8								
Bent-Over Rowing		12		8								
Push-Ups		10		9		8		7		6		5

NAME _____

Exercises: CHEST DEVELOPMENT - Nautilus

	Wt. 1 Reps.	Wt. 2 Reps.	Wt. 3 Reps.	Wt. 4 Reps.	Wt. 5 Reps.
Chest Uppers - Positive	12				
Chest Press - Positive	12				
Multi Ex Dips - Negative	12				
10° Angle Chest	12				
40° Angle Chest	12				

NAME _____

Exercises: CIRCUIT TRAINING

*30 sec. rest between set and station

	Wt. 1 Reps.	Wt. 2 Reps.	Wt. 3 Reps.	Wt. 4 Reps.	Wt. 5 Reps.
Bench	10	8	6		
High Pulls	10	8	6		
Leg Extension	10	8	6		
Leg Curl	10	8	6		
Sit-Ups	10	8	6		
Military Press	10	8	6		
AMF Leg Press	10	8	6		
Lat Pulldown	10	8	0		
Dips	10	8	6		
Jump Rope	60	60	60		

NAME _____

Exercises: HEAVY CIRCUIT

	Wt. 1 Reps.	Wt. 2 Reps.	Wt. 3 Reps.	Wt. 4 Reps.	Wt. 5 Reps.
Bench Press	8	6	4		
Power Pulls	8	6	4		
Squats	8	6	4		
Military Press	8	6	4		
AMF Leg Press	8	6	4		
Leg Curl	15	10			

NAME _____

Exercises: FENCING

TUESDAY	Wt. 1 Reps.	Wt. 2 Reps.	Wt. 3 Reps.	Wt. 4 Reps.	Wt. 5 Reps.
Bench Press	12	8			
High Lat Pull	12	8			
N. Shoulder Press	12	8			
Tricep Pushdown	12	8			
E-Z Bicep Curl	12	8			
Wrist Curls	12	8			
N. Leg Press	12	8			
Ab-Adductor	15				
N. Leg Curl	12	8			
Crunch Machine	15				

THURSDAY

N. Chest Press	12	8			
Chin-Ups	12	8			
Upright Row/Shrugs	12	8			
Close Grip Push Up	12	8			
Str. Bar Bicep	12	8			
Forearm Curls	12	8			
Hip Sled	12	8			
Lunges	12				
N. Leg Curl	10	10			
Weighted Sit-Ups	15	10			

NAME _____

Exercises: FOOTBALL IN SEASON LINEMEN

MONDAY	Wt. 1 Reps.	Wt. 2 Reps.	Wt. 3 Reps.	Wt. 4 Reps.	Wt. 5 Reps.
Bench Press	10	8	6	4	
High Lat Pull	12	8			
Military Press	10	8	6		
Tricep Pushdown	12	8			
Str. Bar Bicep	10	10			
Hip Sled	10	8	6		
Ab-Adductor	15				
Hip Flexer	15				
N. Leg Curl	10	10			
Manual Neck	10	10			

WEDNESDAY					
Incline Bench	10	8	6	4	
Close Grip Lat	10	10	10		
N. Shoulder Press	12	8			
E-Z Tricep Press	10	10			
E-Z Bicep Curl	10	10			
N. Leg Press	15	10			
Lunges	12				
Multi Toe Raises	15	15			
N. Leg Curl	10	10			
Manual Neck	10	10			

FRIDAY					
Bench Press	8	8	8		
E-Z Pullover	10	10			
DB Lateral Raise	12	8			
Weighted Dips	12	8			
Manual Bicep	8				
Leg Extension	10	10			
N. Leg Curl	10	10			
Manual Neck	10	10			

NAME _____

Exercises: FOOTBALL IN SEASON BACKS

MONDAY	Wt. 1 Reps.	Wt. 2 Reps.	Wt. 3 Reps.	Wt. 4 Reps.	Wt. 5 Reps.
Bench Press	12	10	8		
High Lat Pull	12	8			
Military Press	10	8	6		
Tricep Pushdown	12	8			
Str. Bar Bicep	10	10			
Hip Sled	12	8			
N. Leg Curl	10	10			
Manual Neck	10	10			

THURSDAY					
Incline Bench	10	8	6		
Close Grip Lat	12	8			
N. Shoulder Press	12	8			
E-Z Tricep Press	10	10			
E-Z Bicep Curl	10	10			
Leg Extension	12	8			
N. Leg Curl	10	10			
Manual Neck	10	10			

NAME _____

Exercises: FOOTBALL OFF SEASON SPECIAL PROGRAM

MONDAY	Wt. 1 Reps.	Wt. 2 Reps.	Wt. 3 Reps.	Wt. 4 Reps.	Wt. 5 Reps.	Wt. 6 Reps.
Bench Press	7	7	5	5	3	3
DB Incline	10	10				
Weighted Dips	15	10				
DB Deadlift	12					
Leverage Leg Press	12	10	8			
Hip Flexer	12	8				
Lunges	12					
Box Squats	15	15				

TUESDAY

	1	2	3	4	5	6
Military Press	8	7	6	5	4	
DB Lateral Raise	10	10				
Upright Row/Shrugs	8	8				
Close Grip Lat	12	10	8			
E-Z Pullover	15	10				
Tricep Pushdown	10	10	10			
E-Z Bicep Curl	10	10	10			
Close Grip Bench	10	10	10			
4-Way Neck	10	10				

THURSDAY

	1	2	3	4	5	6
Incline Bench	7	7	5	5	3	3
DB Chest Press	10	10				
Weighted Dips	15	10				
Back Squat	8	6	6			
Hip Flexer	15					
Ab-Adductor	15					
Leverage Leg Press	12	8				
Str. Leg Deadlift	15					
Leg Curl	12	10	8			

FRIDAY

	1	2	3	4	5	6
N. Shoulder Press	10	10	10			
DB Lateral Raise	12					
Upright Row/Shrugs	10	8	6			
E-Z Pullover	10	10	10			
High Lat Pulldown	15	10				
E-Z Tricep Press	15					
Str. Bar Bicep	10	10	10			
Close Grip Bench	12	10	8			
Manual Bicep	12					
Manual Neck	10	10				

Exercises: FOOTBALL OFF SEASON HEAVY PROGRAM

MONDAY	Wt. 1 Reps.	Wt. 2 Reps.	Wt. 3 Reps.	Wt. 4 Reps.	Wt. 5 Reps.	Wt. 6 Reps.
Incline Bench	7	7	5	5	3	3
DB Chest Press	10	10				
Weighted Dips	15	10				
Back Squat	8	6	6			
Hip Flexer	15					
Ab-Adductor	15					
Leverage Leg Press	12	8				
Str. Leg Deadlift	15					
Leg Curl	12	10	8			

TUESDAY

N. Shoulder Press	10	10	10			
DB Lateral Raise	12					
Upright Row/Shrugs	10	8	6			
E-Z Pullover	10	10	10			
High Lat Pulldown	15	10				
E-Z Tricep Press	10	10	10			
Str. Bar Bicep	10	10	10			
Close Grip Bench	12	10	8			
Manual Bicep	12					
Manual Neck	10	10				

THURSDAY

Bench Press	7	7	5	5	3	3
DB Incline	10	10				
Weighted Dips	15	10				
DB Deadlift	12					
Leverage Leg Press	12	10	8			
Hip Flexer	12	8				
Lunges	12					
Box Squats	15	15				

FRIDAY

Military Press	8	6	4	4		
DB Lateral Raise	10	10				
Upright Row/Shrugs	8	8				
Close Grip Lat	12	10	8			
E-Z Pullover	15	10				
Tricep Pushdown	10	10	10			
E-Z Bicep Curl	10	10	10			
Close Grip Bench	10	10	10			
4-Way Neck	10	10				

NAME _____

Exercises: GOLF

MONDAY

Exercise	Wt.1	Reps.	Wt.2	Reps.	Wt.3	Reps.	Wt.4	Reps.	Wt.5	Reps.
N. Chest Press		10		10						
Chin-Ups		12								
N. Shoulder Press		12		8						
Tricep Pushdown		10		10						
E-Z Bicep Curl		10		10						
Wrist Curls		15								
N. Leg Press		12		8						
Ab-Adductor		15								
N. Leg Curl		10		10						
Weighted Sit-Ups		15		10						

WEDNESDAY

Exercise	Wt.1	Reps.	Wt.2	Reps.	Wt.3	Reps.	Wt.4	Reps.	Wt.5	Reps.
Bench Press		10		8		6				
Nautilus Pullover		12								
Military Press		10		8						
Weighted Dips		15		10						
Manual Bicep		12								
Forearm Curls		15								
Leverage Leg Press		15		10						
Hip Flexer		15								
N. Leg Curl		12		8						
Crunch Machine		15								

FRIDAY

Exercise	Wt.1	Reps.	Wt.2	Reps.	Wt.3	Reps.	Wt.4	Reps.	Wt.5	Reps.
Incline Bench		10		8		6				
Close Grip Lat		10		10						
DB Lateral Raise		10		10						
Tricep Pushdown		12		8						
E-Z Bicep Curl		12		8						
Wrist Curls		15								
Leg Extension		15		10						
Lunges		12								
N. Leg Curl		10		10						
Weighted Sit-Ups		15		10						

NAME _____

Exercises: GYMNASTICS

	Wt. 1 Reps.	Wt. 2 Reps.	Wt. 3 Reps.	Wt. 4 Reps.	Wt. 5 Reps.
MONDAY					
Incline Bench	12	8			
Chin Ups	12				
N. Shouder Press	12	8			
Tricep Pushdown	10	10			
Str. Bar Bicep	10	10			
Hip Sled	10	10			
Lunges	12				
Multi Toe Raises	10	10			
N. Leg Curl	10	10			
Crunch Machine	15				
Cycling - 8:00					
WEDNESDAY					
N. Chest Press	12	8			
Nautilus Pullover	12	8			
Military Press	12	8			
Weighted Dips	10	10			
E-Z Bicep Curl	10	10			
Leg Extension	12	8			
Ab-Adductor	15				
Multi Toe Raises	10	10			
N. Leg Curl	10	10			
Weighted Sit-Ups	15				
Ball Throws	15				
Cycling - 8:00					
FRIDAY					
Bench Press	12	8			
Close Grip Lat	12				
DB Lateral Raise	8	8			
Tricep Pushdown	12	8			
Manual Bicep	10				
N. Leg Press	12	8			
Hip Flexer	15				
Multi Toe Raises	10	10			
N. Leg Curl	10	10			
Crunch Machine	15				
Cycling - 8:00					

NAME _____

Exercises: HIKING - Free Weight & Universal

	Wt. 1 Reps.	Wt. 2 Reps.	Wt. 3 Reps.	Wt. 4 Reps.	Wt. 5 Reps.
Squats	8	6	4	2	1
Universal Leg Extension	15				
Universal Leg Press	15				
Leg Curl	15				
Toe Raises	12	12	12		
Step-Ups	12	12			
Jump Rope	250				
Sit-Ups	50	25	25		

NAME _____

Exercises: HIKING - Nautilus

	Wt. 1 Reps.	Wt. 2 Reps.	Wt. 3 Reps.	Wt. 4 Reps.	Wt. 5 Reps.
Compound Leg	15	15			
Leg Curl	15	10			
Multi Ex Squats	12	8			
Calf Raise	12	12	12		
Ab-Adductor	12				
Low-Back	15				
Rotary Torso	15				
Crunches	15				
Side Bend - Multi Ex.	15				

NAME _____

Exercises: HIPS - Free Weight & Universal

	Wt. 1 Reps.	Wt. 2 Reps.	Wt. 3 Reps.	Wt. 4 Reps.	Wt. 5 Reps.
Squats	10	10	10	8	8
Universal Leg Press	15				
Universal Leg Extension	15				
Universal Leg Curl	15				
Side Leg Raises	15	15			
Crunches	12				
Step-Ups	20	15			
Universal Ab-Adductor	25	25			
Side Bends	25	25			
Sit-Ups	25				

NAME _____

Exercises: HIPS - Nautilus	Wt. 1 Reps.	Wt. 2 Reps.	Wt. 3 Reps.	Wt. 4 Reps.	Wt. 5 Reps.
Dupoly Hip & Back	15				
Leg Press	15				
Leg Curl	15				
Leg Extension	15				
Multi Ex. Squats	12	8			
Ab-Adductor	15	15			

NAME _____

Exercises: HIP & THIGH REDUCTION - Free Weight & Universal										
	Wt. 1	Reps.	Wt. 2	Reps.	Wt. 3	Reps.	Wt. 4	Reps.	Wt. 5	Reps.
Squats		10		10		8		8		8
Universal Leg Extension		15								
Universal Leg Press		15								
Universal Leg Curls		15								
Lat Leg Raises - Low Pulley		15		15						
Side Bends		15		15						
Leg Lifts		15								
Straight-Legged Dead Lift		12								
Sit-Ups		25								

NAME _____

Exercises: HOCKEY IN SEASON

TUESDAY	Wt. 1 Reps.	Wt. 2 Reps.	Wt. 3 Reps.	Wt. 4 Reps.	Wt. 5 Reps.
Bench Press	12	10	8		
Close Grip Lat	12	8			
Military Press	12	8			
Multi Ex Dips	10	10			
Str. Bar Bicep	10	10			
Hip Sled	10	8	6		
Lunges	12				
N. Leg Curl	10	10			
Crunch Machine	15				

THURSDAY

	Wt. 1 Reps.	Wt. 2 Reps.	Wt. 3 Reps.	Wt. 4 Reps.	Wt. 5 Reps.
Incline Bench	10	8	8		
High Lat Pull	12	8			
N. Shoulder Press	12	8			
Tricep Pushdown	10	10			
E-Z Bicep Curl	10	10			
N. Leg Press	12	8			
Lunges	12				
N. Leg Curl	10	10			
Weighted Sit-Ups	15				

NAME _____

Exercises: HOCKEY OFF SEASON

MONDAY

Exercise	1 Wt/Reps	2 Wt/Reps	3 Wt/Reps	4 Wt/Reps	5 Wt/Reps
Bench Press	10	10	10		
Close Grip Lat	10	10			
N. Shoulder Press	12	8			
Multi Ex Dips	10	8			
E-Z Bicep Curl	15	10			
Leverage Leg Press	15	10			
Ab-Adductor	15				
Multi Toe Raises	15	15			
N. Leg Curl	15	10			
N. Abdominal	15				

WEDNESDAY

Exercise	1 Wt/Reps	2 Wt/Reps	3 Wt/Reps	4 Wt/Reps	5 Wt/Reps
Incline Bench	10	10	10		
High Lat Pull	12	8			
Military Press	10	10			
Tricep Pushdown	15	10			
E-Z Bicep Curl	10	10			
N. Leg Press	12	8			
Lunges	15				
Multi Toe Raises	15	15			
N. Leg Curl	12	8			
Ball Throw - 25					

FRIDAY

Exercise	1 Wt/Reps	2 Wt/Reps	3 Wt/Reps	4 Wt/Reps	5 Wt/Reps
Bench Press	12	10	8		
Close Grip Lat	15	10			
N. Shoulder Press	15	10			
Multi Ex Dips	12	8			
E-Z Bicep Curl	12	8			
Leverage Leg Press	10	10			
Hip Flexer	15				
Multi Toe Raises	15	15			
N. Leg Curl	10	10			
N. Abdominal	15				

NAME _____

Exercises: JOGGING - Free Weight & Universal

	Wt. 1 Reps.	Wt. 2 Reps.	Wt. 3 Reps.	Wt. 4 Reps.	Wt. 5 Reps.
Bench	10	10	10		
Dips	12				
Lateral Raises Dumbbell	12				
Lat Pulldown	12				
Chin-Ups	12				
Reverse Curls	12				
Universal Leg Extension	15				
Universal Leg Press	15				
Universal Leg Curl	15				
Toe Raises	12	12	12		

NAME _____

Exercises: LACROSSE

MONDAY	Wt. 1 Reps.	Wt. 2 Reps.	Wt. 3 Reps.	Wt. 4 Reps.	Wt. 5 Reps.
Bench Press	7	5	4	3	2
High Lat Pull	10	8	6		
Military Press	10	8	6		
Tricep Pushdown	10	8	8		
E-Z Bicep Curl	10	8	6		
Back Squat	8	6	4	4	
Ab-Adductor	15				
Hip Sled Toe Raise	15	15			
N. Leg Curl	10	8	6		
Weighted Sit-Ups	15	15			

WEDNESDAY

Exercise	1	2	3	4	5
Incline Bench	7	5	5	3	
Chin-Ups	10	8	6		
N. Shoulder Press	15	10			
DB Lateral Raise	12				
Weighted Dips	15	10			
Manual Bicep Curl	12				
DB Bicep Curl	8	8			
Hip Sled	12	10	8		
Hip Flexer	15				
Hip Sled Toe Raise	15	15			
N. Leg Curl	15	10			
Roman Twist	15	10			

FRIDAY

Exercise	1	2	3	4	5
Bench Press	5	5	5	3	3
Close Grip Lat	12	10	8		
DB Lateral Raise	10	8			
Upright Row/Shrugs	15				
E-Z Tricep Press	10	8	8		
Str. Bar Bicep	10	10	10		
N. Leg Press	15	10			
Lunges	12				
Hip Sled Toe Raise	15	15			
N. Leg Curl	12	8			
Weighted Sit-Ups	15	15			

NAME _____

Exercises: MARTIAL ARTS - Nautilus										
	Wt. 1	Reps.	Wt. 2	Reps.	Wt. 3	Reps.	Wt. 4	Reps.	Wt. 5	Reps.
Compound Leg Extension Neg.		15								
Compound Leg Press - Neg.		15								
Leg Curl - Negative		15								
Hip & Back (Dupoly)		12								
Pullover - Negative		12								
Chin-Up - Multi Ex - Neg.		12								
Shoulder Flys - Negative		12								
Shoulder Press - Negative		12								
Dips Multi Ex - Neg.		12								
Multi Ex. Forearms		12								
Multi Ex. Side Bends		12		12						
Ab - Adductor		12		12						
Stiff - Legged Bend Lift		12								

NAME _____

Exercises: MIDDLE AGE FITNESS - Free Weight & Universal

	Wt. 1 Reps.	Wt. 2 Reps.	Wt. 3 Reps.	Wt. 4 Reps.	Wt. 5 Reps.
Universal Bench	12	10	8	6	4
Dumbbell Chest Flys	12	8			
Dumbbell Lateral Raises	12	8			
Side Bends	12	8			
Sit-Ups	12	8			
Push-Ups	12	8			
Universal Leg Extension	12	8			
Universal Curls	12	8			

NAME _____

Exercises: MIDDLE AGE FITNESS - Nautilus										
	Wt. 1	Reps.	Wt. 2	Reps.	Wt. 3	Reps.	Wt. 4	Reps.	Wt. 5	Reps.
Compound Leg		15		15						
Leg Curl		12								
Ab-Adductor		12		12						
Multi Ext. Toe Raises		12								
Double Chest		12		12						
Pullover		12		12						
Double Shoulder		12		8						
Multi Ex. Side Bends		12		8						
Sit-Ups		12		8						

NAME _____

Exercises: MUSCLE TONE - Free Weight & Universal

Exercise	Wt.	1 Reps.	Wt.	2 Reps.	Wt.	3 Reps.	Wt.	4 Reps.	Wt.	5 Reps.	Wt.	6 Reps.
Bench		10		8		8		8		6		4
Dumbbell Incline Press		12										
Dumbbell Lateral Raises		12										
Sitting Military		12										
Lateral Pulldown		12										
Pull-Ups		12										
Triceps Ext.		12										
Biceps Curls		12										
Universal Leg Extension		15										
Universal Leg Press		15										
Universal Leg Curls		15										

NAME _____

Exercises: **MUSCLE TONE - Nautilus**										
	Wt. **1**	Reps.	Wt. **2**	Reps.	Wt. **3**	Reps.	Wt. **4**	Reps.	Wt. **5**	Reps.
Hip & Back (Dupoly)		12								
Compound Leg Extension		15								
Compound Leg Press		15								
Leg Curls		15								
Chest Uppers		12								
Chest Press		12								
Shoulder Flys		12								
Shoulder Press		12								
Pullover		12								
Pulldown		12								
Multi Ex. Dips		12								
Multi Ex. Chin		12								

NAME _____

Exercises: SKIING - Free Weight & Universal

	Wt. 1 Reps.	Wt. 2 Reps.	Wt. 3 Reps.	Wt. 4 Reps.	Wt. 5 Reps.
Squats	10	10	8	8	6
Stiff-Legged Deadlift	12				
Universal Leg Extension	15				
Universal Leg Curl	15				
Universal Leg Press	15				
Chin-Ups	12	8			
Dips	12	8			
Sitting Military	8	6			
Dumbbell Side Bends	25	25			
Toe Raises	12	12	12		
Sit-Ups	25	25	25		

NAME _____

Exercises: SKIING - Nautilus										
	Wt. 1	Reps.	Wt. 2	Reps.	Wt. 3	Reps.	Wt. 4	Reps.	Wt. 5	Reps.
Hip & Back (Dupoly)		12								
Leg. Extension		15								
Leg Curl		15								
Leg Press		15								
Chin-Ups		12								
Dip		12								
Shoulder Press		12								
Side Bend - Multi Ex.		15		15						
4-Way Neck		8-8		8-8						
Sit-Ups		23		23		23				

NAME _____

Exercises: SOCCER IN SEASON

TUESDAY	Wt. 1 Reps.	Wt. 2 Reps.	Wt. 3 Reps.	Wt. 4 Reps.	Wt. 5 Reps.
Bench Press	12	8			
Close Grip Lat	12	8			
N. Shoulder Press	15				
Tricep Pushdown	10	10			
E-Z Bicep Curl	10	10			
Hip Sled	10	10			
Ab-Adductor	15				
N. Leg Curl	10	10			
Crunch Machine	15				

THURSDAY					
N. Chest Press	12	8			
Nautilus Pullover	12	8			
N. Shoulder Fly	12	8			
Multi Ex Dips	10	10			
Str. Bar Bicep	10	10			
N. Leg Press	12	8			
Lunges	12				
N. Leg Curl	10	10			
Weighted Sit-Ups	15				

NAME _____

Exercises: SOCCER OFF SEASON										
MONDAY	Wt. 1	Reps.	Wt. 2	Reps.	Wt. 3	Reps.	Wt. 4	Reps.	Wt. 5	Reps.
Bench Press		10		8		6				
Close Grip Lat		8		8		8				
N. Shoulder Press		10		10						
Tricep Pushdown		10		10						
E-Z Bicep Curl		10		10						
Leverage Leg Press		10		10						
Lunges		12								
N. Leg Curl		15		10						
N. Abdominal		15								
WEDNESDAY										
Incline Bench		10		10		10				
High Lat Pull		8		8						
Military Press		10		10						
Multi Ex Dips		15		10						
Str. Bar Bicep		15		10						
N. Leg Press		10		10						
Hip Flexer		15								
N. Leg Curl		12		8						
Ball Throw		15		15						
FRIDAY										
Bench Press		12		10		8				
Close Grip Lat		8		8						
N. Shoulder Press		12		8						
Tricep Pushdown		8		8						
E-Z Bicep Curl		15		10						
Leverage Leg Press		12		8						
Ab-Adductor		15								
N. Leg Curl		10		10						
N. Abdominal		15								

NAME _____

Exercises: SOFTBALL

MONDAY

Exercise	Wt.1	Reps.	Wt.2	Reps.	Wt.3	Reps.	Wt.4	Reps.	Wt.5	Reps.
N. Chest Press		12		8						
Nautilus Pullover		12								
Military Press		12		8						
Weighted Dips		10		10						
Manual Bicep		10								
N. Leg Press		12		8						
Ab-Adductor		15								
N. Leg Curl		10		10						
Weighted Sit-Ups		15								

WEDNESDAY

Exercise	Wt.1	Reps.	Wt.2	Reps.	Wt.3	Reps.	Wt.4	Reps.	Wt.5	Reps.
Bench Press		12		8						
Close Grip Lat		12								
DB Lateral Raise		8		8						
Tricep Pushdown		12		8						
Str. Bar Bicep		10		10						
Hip Sled		10		10						
Hip Flexer		15								
N. Leg Curl		10		10						
Crunch Machine		15								

FRIDAY

Exercise	Wt.1	Reps.	Wt.2	Reps.	Wt.3	Reps.	Wt.4	Reps.	Wt.5	Reps.
Incline Bench		12		8						
Chin-Ups		12								
N. Shoulder Press		12		8						
Weighted Dips		10		10						
E-Z Bicep Curl		10		10						
Leg Extension		12		8						
Lunges		12								
N. Leg Curl		10		10						
Weighted Sit-Ups		15								

NAME _____

Exercises: SWIMMING

MONDAY

Exercise	Wt.1	Reps.	Wt.2	Reps.	Wt.3	Reps.	Wt.4	Reps.	Wt.5	Reps.
Bench Press		12		10		8				
High Lat Pull		12		8						
N. Shoulder Press		15		10						
Tricep Pushdown		12		8						
E-Z Bicep Curl		10		10						
Hip Sled		15		10						
Ab-Adductor		15								
Multi Toe Raises		15		15						
N. Leg Curl		12		8						
Crunch Machine		15								
Ball Throws		15		15						

WEDNESDAY

Exercise	Wt.1	Reps.	Wt.2	Reps.	Wt.3	Reps.	Wt.4	Reps.	Wt.5	Reps.
Military Press		10		10		10				
Chin-Ups		12		8						
Bench Press		8		8		8				
E-Z Tricep Press		10		10						
Str. Bar Bicep		12		8						
N. Leg Press		15		10						
Lunges		12								
Multi Toe Raises		15		15						
N. Leg Curl		10		10						
Weighted Sit-Ups		15		15						
Ball Throws		15		15						

FRIDAY

Exercise	Wt.1	Reps.	Wt.2	Reps.	Wt.3	Reps.	Wt.4	Reps.	Wt.5	Reps.
Incline Bench		10		8		8				
E-Z Pullover		10		10						
Upright Row/Shrugs		10		10						
Weighted Dips		15		10						
Manual Bicep		8								
Hip Sled		10		10						
Hip Flexer		15								
Multi Toe Raises		15		15						
N. Leg Curl		12		8						
Crunch Machine		15								
Ball Throws		15		15						

NAME _____

Exercises: DISTANCE SWIMMING										
	Wt. 1	Reps.	Wt. 2	Reps.	Wt. 3	Reps.	Wt. 4	Reps.	Wt. 5	Reps.
Pullover		24		24		24				
Dips - Maximum		2 pos.								
Chins - Maximum		2 pos.								
Triceps Ext.		24		24		24				
Medicine Ball		100		100		100				

NAME _____

Exercises: SWIMMING MIDDLE DISTANCE

	1 Wt. / Reps.	2 Wt. / Reps.	3 Wt. / Reps.	4 Wt. / Reps.	5 Wt. / Reps.
Double Chest	24	8	24		
Pullover	24	8	24		
Dips - Maximum	1 Pos.	1 Neg.			
Chins - Maximum	1 Pos.	1 Neg.			
Triceps Ext.	2x16	1x8	2x16		
Lat Pulldowns	24	8	24		
Ab-Adductor	24	24	24		
Medicine Ball	100	100	100		

NAME _____

Exercises: SWIMMING SPRINTERS

	1 Wt. Reps.	2 Wt. Reps.	3 Wt. Reps.	4 Wt. Reps.	5 Wt. Reps.
Double Chest	16	8	16		
Pullover	16	8	16		
Dips - Maximum	1 Pos.	1 Neg.			
Chins - Maximum	1 Pos.	1 Neg.			
Triceps Ext.	2x12	1x8	2x12		
Lat Pulldowns	16	8	16		
Ab-Adductor	16	16	16		
Medicine Ball	100	100	100		

NAME _____

Exercises: TENNIS										
TUESDAY	Wt.1	Reps.	Wt.2	Reps.	Wt.3	Reps.	Wt.4	Reps.	Wt.5	Reps.
Bench Press		12		8						
Close Grip Lat		12		8						
N. Shoulder Press		15								
Tricep Pushdown		10		10						
E-Z Bicep Curl		10		10						
Hip Sled		10		10						
Ab-Adductor		15								
N. Leg Curl		10		10						
Weighted Sit-Ups		15								
THURSDAY										
N. Chest Press		12		8						
Nautilus Pullover		12		8						
N. Shoulder Fly		12		8						
Multi Ex Dips		10		10						
Str. Bar Bicep		10		10						
N. Leg Press		12		8						
Lunges		12								
N. Leg Curl		10		10						
Crunch Machine		15								

NAME _____

Exercises: TRACK IN SEASON

TUESDAY	Wt. 1 Reps.	Wt. 2 Reps.	Wt. 3 Reps.	Wt. 4 Reps.	Wt. 5 Reps.
Bench Press	12	10	8		
Chin-Ups	12	8			
Military Press	12	8			
Multi Ex Dips	10	10			
Str. Bar Bicep	10	10			
Hip Sled	10	8	6		
Hip Flexer	15				
Lunges	12				
Multi Toe Raises	15	15			
N. Leg Curl	10	10			
Crunch Machine	15				

THURSDAY

Exercise	1	2	3	4	5
Incline Bench	10	8	8		
High Lat Pull	12	8			
N. Shoulder Press	12	8			
Tricep Pushdown	10	10			
E-Z Bicep Curl	10	10			
Back Squat	12	8			
Ab-Adductor	15				
Lunges	12				
Multi Toe Raises	15	15			
N. Leg Curl	10	10			
Weighted Sit-Ups	15				

NAME _____

Exercises: TRACK OFF SEASON

MONDAY	Wt. 1 Reps.	Wt. 2 Reps.	Wt. 3 Reps.	Wt. 4 Reps.	Wt. 5 Reps.	Wt. 6 Reps.
Bench Press	5	5	5	3	3	
Incline Bench	7	5	3			
Back Squat	6	5	4	3		
Hip Flexer	15					
Lunges (Alt. Legs)	12					
Hip Sled	7	5	3			
Deadlift	7	5	3			
Weighted Sit-Ups	15	15				

TUESDAY

	Wt. 1 Reps.	Wt. 2 Reps.	Wt. 3 Reps.	Wt. 4 Reps.	Wt. 5 Reps.	Wt. 6 Reps.
Behind Neck Press	7	5	3			
Upright Row/Shrugs	8	8				
Chin Ups	15	15				
High Lat Pull	8	6	6			
Tricep Pushdown	8	6	6			
Man. Tricep Press	12					
Str. Bar Bicep	8	8	8			
Manual Bicep Curl	10					
Wrist Curls	15	15				

THURSDAY

	Wt. 1 Reps.	Wt. 2 Reps.	Wt. 3 Reps.	Wt. 4 Reps.	Wt. 5 Reps.	Wt. 6 Reps.
Incline Bench	5	5	5	3	3	
Bench Press	7	5	3			
Power Clean	7	5	3			
Hip Flexer	15					
Lunges (Alt. Legs)	12					
Hip Sled	8	6	4			
Str. Leg Deadlift	12					

FRIDAY

	Wt. 1 Reps.	Wt. 2 Reps.	Wt. 3 Reps.	Wt. 4 Reps.	Wt. 5 Reps.	Wt. 6 Reps.
Behind Neck Press	8	6	4			
Upright Row/Shrugs	12	8				
Bent Over Row	8	6	4			
Bent Arm Pullover	8	6	6			
Tricep Pushdown	8	8				
Man. Tricep Press	8					
Str. Bar Bicep	8	8				
Manual Bicep Curl	8					
Wrist Curls	15					
Weighted Sit-Ups	15	15				

NAME _____

Exercises: VOLLEYBALL IN SEASON

MONDAY	Wt. 1 Reps.	Wt. 2 Reps.	Wt. 3 Reps.	Wt. 4 Reps.	Wt. 5 Reps.
Incline Bench	12	8			
Nautilus Pullover	12				
Military Press	8	8			
Multi Ex Dips	12				
Str. Bar Bicep	12	8			
Hip Sled	12	8			
Hip Flexer	15				
Multi Toe Raises	15	15			
N. Leg Curl	12	8			
Crunch Machine	15				

THURSDAY					
Bench Press	12	8			
High Lat Pull	12	8			
N. Shoulder Press	12	8			
Tricep Pushdown	12	8			
E-Z Bicep Curl	12	8			
N. Leg Press	12	8			
Ab-Adductor	15				
Multi Toe Raises	15	15			
N. Leg Curl	15	10			
Weighted Sit-Ups	15	15			

NAME _____

Exercises: VOLLEYBALL OFF SEASON

TUESDAY	Wt. 1 Reps.	Wt. 2 Reps.	Wt. 3 Reps.	Wt. 4 Reps.	Wt. 5 Reps.
Bench Press	10	8	6		
Close Grip Lat	15	10			
Military Press	8	8	6		
Multi Ex Dips	15	10			
E-Z Bicep Curl	15	10			
Leverage Leg Press	10	10			
Ab-Adductor	15				
Multi Toe Raises	15	15			
N. Leg Curl	10	10			
N. Abdominal	15	10			

THURSDAY

Exercise	1	2	3	4	5
Incline Bench	10	10	10		
High Lat Pull	15	10			
N. Shoulder Press	10	10			
Tricep Pushdown	12	8			
Manual Bicep	8				
N. Leg Press	12	8			
Hip Flexer	15				
Multi Toe Raises	15	15			
N. Leg Curl	15	10			
Ball Throw - 25					

SATURDAY

Exercise	1	2	3	4	5
Bench Press	8	6	4		
Close Grip Lat	10	10			
Military Press	8	8	8		
Multi Ex Dips	10	10			
E-Z Bicep Curl	12	8			
Leverage Leg Press	12	8			
Lunges	12				
Multi Toe Raises	15	15			
N. Leg Curl	12	8			
N. Abdominal	15	10			

NAME _____

Exercises: WEIGHT GAIN - Free Weight & Universal

Exercise	1 Wt./Reps.	2 Wt./Reps.	3 Wt./Reps.	4 Wt./Reps.	5 Wt./Reps.
Bench	6	4	2	1	
Dumbbell Incline	8	6	4		
Sitting Military	8	6	4		
High Pull	8	6	4		
Biceps/Curls	8	6			
Triceps Ext.	8	6			
Squats	8	6	4		
Universal Leg Extension	15				
Universal Leg Press	15				
Universal Leg Curls	15				

NAME _____

Exercises: WEIGHT GAIN - Nautilus

	Wt. 1 Reps.	Wt. 2 Reps.	Wt. 3 Reps.	Wt. 4 Reps.	Wt. 5 Reps.
Chest Upper	8-12				
Chest Press	8-12				
Shoulder Flys	8-12				
Shoulder Press	8-12				
Pullover	8-12				
Pulldown	8-12				
Multi Ex. Dips (Weight)	8-12				
Multi Ex. Chins (Weight)	8-12				
Compound Leg Press	12				
Compound Leg Extension	12				
Leg Curls	12				

NAME _____

Exercises: WEIGHT LOSS - Free Weight & Universal										
	Wt. 1	Reps.	Wt. 2	Reps.	Wt. 3	Reps.	Wt. 4	Reps.	Wt. 5	Reps.
Bench		12		12		12				
Dumbbell Chest Flys		18								
Dumbbell Lat Raises		18								
Lateral Pulldown		18								
Dumbbell Side Bends		18		18						
Universal Leg Extension		18								
Universal Leg Press		18								
Universal Leg Curls		18								
Low Pulley Lat Raises		18		18						
Sit-Ups		50								
Jump Rope		5 Mins.								

NAME _____

Exercises: WEIGHT LOSS - Nautilus

	Wt. 1 Reps.	Wt. 2 Reps.	Wt. 3 Reps.	Wt. 4 Reps.	Wt. 5 Reps.
Chest Upper	18				
Shoulder Flys	18				
Pullover	18				
Multi Ex. Side Bends	18				
Dips	18				
Leg Extension	18				
Leg Press	18				
Leg Curls	18				
Ab-Adductor	18	18			
Sit-Ups	50				
Jump Rope	5 Mins.				

NAME _____

Exercises: WRESTLING

MONDAY	Wt. 1 Reps.	Wt. 2 Reps.	Wt. 3 Reps.	Wt. 4 Reps.	Wt. 5 Reps.
Bench Press	8	6	4	4	
High Lat Pull	12	10	8		
DB Lateral Raise	12	8			
Tricep Pushdown	10	10	10		
E-Z Bicep Curl	10	10	10		
Back Squat	10	8	6		
Ab-Adductor	15				
N. Leg Curl	15	10			
Crunch Machine	15	10			

WEDNESDAY

Incline Bench	10	8	6	4	
Chin-Ups	15	10			
N. Shoulder Press	12	8			
Weighted Dips	15	10			
Manual Bicep Curl	12	8			
N. Leg Press	12	8			
Hip Flexer	15				
N. Leg Curl	15	10			
Weighted Sit-Ups	15	10			

FRIDAY

Bench Press	10	8	6	4	
E-Z Pullover	10	10	10		
Military Press	10	8	6		
Upright Row/Shrugs	12	8			
E-Z Tricep Press	10	10	10		
Str. Bar Bicep	10	10	10		
Hip Sled	15	10			
Lunges	12				
N. Leg Curl	15	10			
Crunch Machine	15	10			

A LIST OF WEIGHT TRAINING REFERENCES

Barrilleaux, D., and Murray, Jim, *Inside Weight Training For Women,* Contemporary Books, Chicago, Ill.

Columbu, Franco, *Winning Weight Lifting and Power Lifting,* Contemporary Press, Chicago, Ill.

Darden, Ellington, *Strength-Training Principles,* Anna Publishing Co., Winter Park, Fla.

Darden, Ellington, *How Your Muscles Work — Featuring Nautilus Training Equipment,* Anna Publishing Co., Winter Park, Fla.

Dobbins, W., Sprague, K., *Golds Gym Weight Training Book,* Berkley Books, New York.

Murray, Jim, *Contemporary Weight Training,* Contemporary Books, Chicago, Ill.

Murray, Jim, *Inside Weight Lifting and Weight Training,* Contemporary Books Inc., Chicago, Ill.

Nagy, George, *Weight Lifting Handbook,* Amateur Athletic Union of the United States, Indianapolis.

Parker, R., and Marsh, J., *Training With Weights,* Sports Illustrated — Lippincott Co.

Stokes, R., Moore, A., Moore, C., Williams, C., *Fitness: The New Wave,* Hunter Publishing Co., Winston-Salem, N.C.

MAGAZINES AND PERIODICALS

Iron Man Magazine, 512 Black Hills Ave., Alliance, Nebraska 69301 (Articles dealing with women who weight train).

Muscle Builder/Power, 21100 Erwin St., Woodland Hills, California 91364.

Muscular Development, P.O. Box 1707, York, PA. 17405.

Muscle Digest, 1234 South Garfield Ave., Alhombra, Claif. 91801.

Muscle Training Illustrated, 1665 Utica Ave., Brooklyn, N.Y. 11234.

Muscle Magazine International, Unit One, 270 Rutherford Road, Brampton, Ontario, Canada.

Strength and Health Magazine, P.O. Box 1707, York, PA 17405. (Has regular features such as "For Women Only" and a "To The Ladies Column.")

Appendix A: References

MUSCLES OF THE BODY

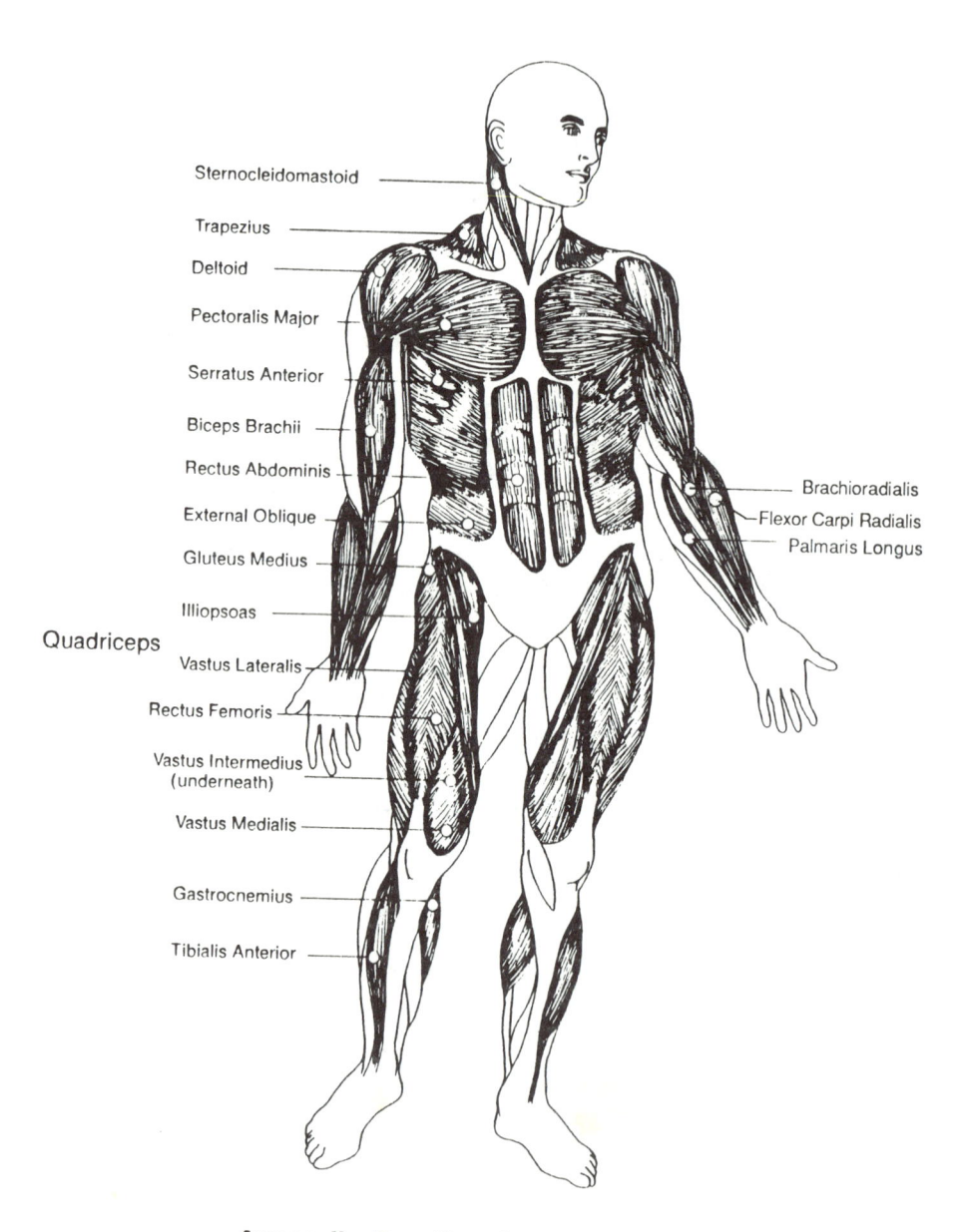

- Sternocleidomastoid
- Trapezius
- Deltoid
- Pectoralis Major
- Serratus Anterior
- Biceps Brachii
- Rectus Abdominis
- External Oblique
- Gluteus Medius
- Illiopsoas
- Quadriceps
- Vastus Lateralis
- Rectus Femoris
- Vastus Intermedius (underneath)
- Vastus Medialis
- Gastrocnemius
- Tibialis Anterior
- Brachioradialis
- Flexor Carpi Radialis
- Palmaris Longus

Appendix B: Muscles of the Body

MUSCLES OF THE BODY

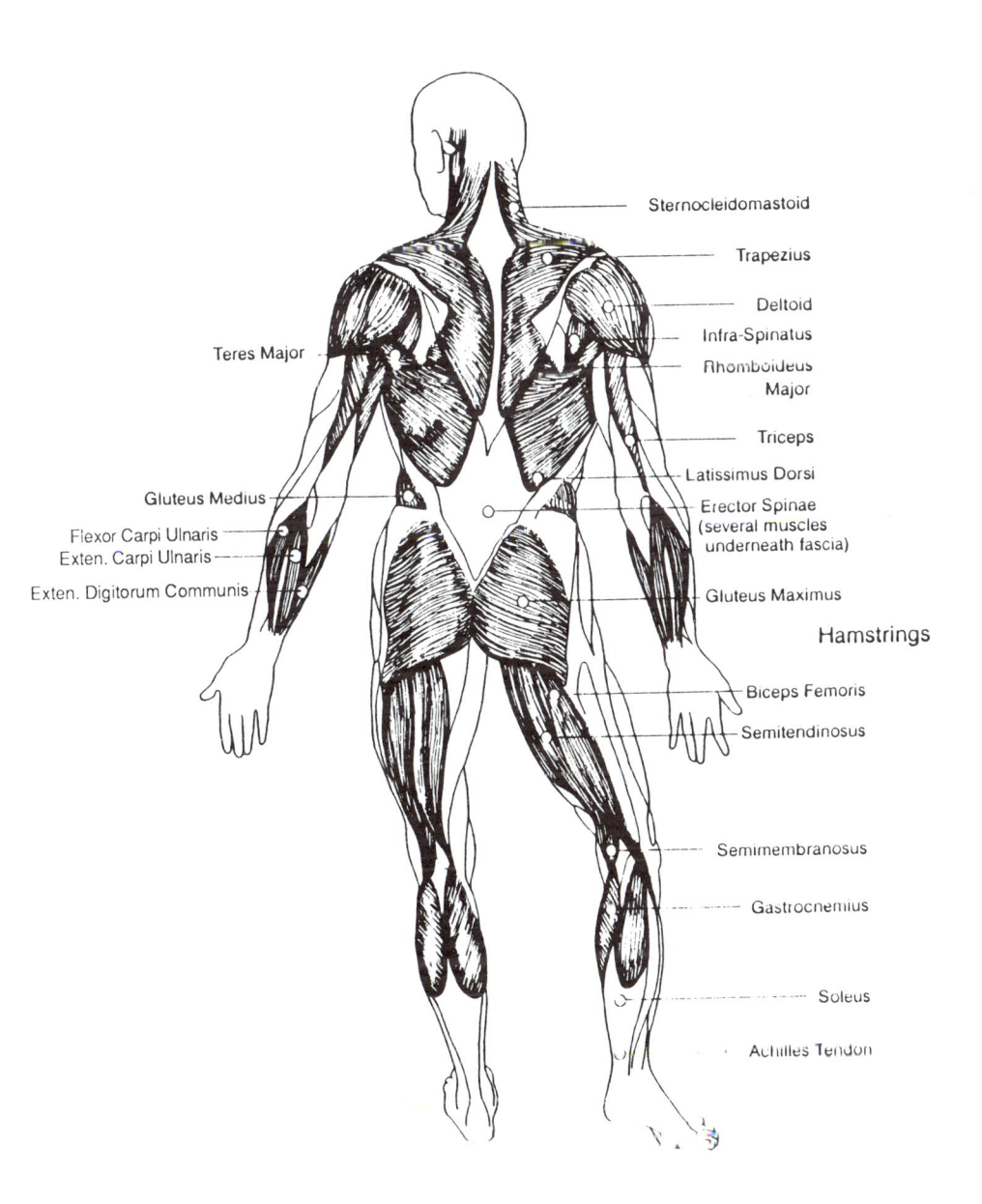

Appendix B: Muscles of the Body

Kilo/Pound Conversion Table

Kilos are converted to pounds by multiplying by 2.2046. A.A.U. weightlifting rules stipulate that pounds shall be rounded off by reducing to the nearest quarter pound. For example: 120 kilos multiplied by 2.2046 = 264.552. Translated into pounds it thus becomes 264½ pounds.

Kilos	Pounds	Kilos	Pounds	Kilos	Pounds
5	11	197.5	435¼	297.5	655¾
10	22	200.0	440¾	300.0	661½
15	33	202.5	446¼	302.5	666¾
20	44	205.0	451¾	305.0	672¼
25	55	207.5	457¼	307.5	677¾
30	66¼	210.0	462¾	310.0	683¼
35	77¼	212.5	468¼	312.5	688¾
40	88¼	215.0	473¾	315.0	694¼
45	99¼	217.5	479½	317.5	699¾
50	110¼	220.0	485	320.0	705¼
55	121¼	222.5	490½	322.5	710¾
60	132¼	225.0	496	325.0	716¼
65	143½	227.5	501½	327.5	722
70	154½	230.0	507	330.0	727½
75	165½	232.5	512½	332.5	733
80	176½	235.0	518	335.0	738½
85	187½	237.5	523½	337.5	744
90	198½	240.0	529	340.0	749½
95	209½	242.5	534½	342.5	755
100	220½	245.0	540	345.0	760½
105	231½	247.5	545½	347.5	766
110	242½	250.0	551	350.0	771½
115	253½	252.5	556½	352.5	777
120	264½	255.0	562	355.0	782½
125	275½	257.5	567½	357.5	788
130	286½	260.0	573	360.0	793½
135	297½	262.5	578½	362.5	799
140	308¾	265.0	584	365.0	804½
145	319¾	267.5	589½	367.5	810
150	330¾	270.0	595	370.0	815½
155	341¾	272.5	600¾	372.5	821
160	352¾	275.0	606¼	375.0	826½
165	363¾	277.5	611¾	377.5	832
170	374¾	280.0	617¼	380.0	837½
175	385¾	282.5	622¾	382.5	843¼
180	396¾	285.0	628¼	385.0	848¾
185	407¾	287.5	633¾	387.5	854¼
187.5	413¼	290.0	639¼	390.0	859¾
190.0	418¾	292.5	644¾	392.5	865¼
192.5	424¼	295.0	650¼	395.0	870¾
195.0	429¾				

_____ Appendix C: Kilo/Pound Conversion Chart _____

Name _____   Date _____

Chapter 1: Weight Training Everyone

1. List three reasons why weight training may be your "cup of tea."

2. What are 5 of the 6 categories of weight trainers?

3. Name the man most responsible for correcting misconceptions about weight training. Hint: He was a medical doctor.

4. Define the following terms:

    a. Extension

    b. Flexion

    c. Hypertrophy

    d. Negative exercise

    e. Sticking point

    f. Overloading

    g. Isometric

——————— Appendix D: Chapter Evaluations ———————

Name _____ Date _____

Chapter 2: Equipment

1. List two advantages of using dumbbells.

2. Plastic covered loose weights are recommended because:

3. Weight training is based on _____ _____.

4. What is the primary value of the incline bench?

5. Leg press machines primarily utilize most of the muscles of:

6. What is the primary advantage of using a "Lat Machine"?

_____ Appendix D: Chapter Evaluations _____

Name _____   Date _____

Chapter 3: Questions Most Often Asked

1. The most powerful muscles of the upper body are:

2. The primary muscles used in running and jumping are:

3. What is the function of the sternocleidomastoid?

4. Is there one muscle in the body more efficient than the others?

5. What is the best way to increase bulk and strength?

6. List the negative aspects of smoking and weight training.

7. Define a "balanced diet."

_____ Appendix D: Chapter Evaluations _____

Name _____   Date _____

Chapter 4: Scientific Principles

1. The amount of work which a person can do and how long he/she can do it is dependent upon:

2. Slow-twitch muscle fibers are characterized by:

3. Define the "all or none principle".

4. List the three major types of muscles found in the body.

5. List three types of muscle contraction.

6. The absorption of oxygen from the blood into the muscle cells is made possible by a substance called _____.

7. Your particular ratio of fast-twitch and slow-twitch fibers is determined _____.

_____ Appendix D: Chapter Evaluations _____

Name _____   Date _____

Chapter 5: Stretching and Avoiding Injury

1. Why should you use a lighter than normal workload during the first four to six workouts?

2. List the benefits of a warm-up prior to heavy work.

3. Name the three basic techniques for passively increasing flexibility.

4. List five general guidelines for a flexibility program.

_____Appendix D: Chapter Evaluations_____

Name _____ Date _____

Chapter 6: Basic Fundamentals

1. Describe the basic stance.

2. Describe the position of your hands when grasping a bar.

3. How do you determine how much weight to begin with?

4. What should be the frequency of your workout?

5. Muscle size will be dependent upon:

_____ _____Appendix D: Chapter Evaluations_____

Name _____ Date _____

Chapter 7: Establishing Your Program

1. Define "overload."

2. List the steps necessary to establish an individualized weight training program.

3. By using the master Muscle Chart, determine the exercises needed to develop the pectoralis majors using free weights and multi-station equipment.

4. Give the general, rule-of-thumb formula for developing strength and bulk as opposed to endurance.

_____ Appendix D: Chapter Evaluations _____

Name _____   Date _____

Chapter 8: Free Weight Lifts

1. One of the best exercises to eliminate or prevent a "dowager's hump" is the _____ _____ .

2. One of the most effective lifts used to develop the front part of the deltoid muscles is the _____ _____ (freeweights).

3. When using free weights, the pectoral chest muscles can be improved best by doing the _____ _____ .

4. List the two best exercises to use with free weights when the back part or under portion of the arm requires development.

5. Racket sports players wishing to improve grip and wrist strength would do well to work on these three exercises.

_____ Appendix D: Chapter Evaluations _____

Name _____ Date _____

Chapter 9: The Universal Machine

Match the following Universal machine exercises to the appropriate muscle or group of muscles.

_____ Leg extension   a. Hamstrings
_____ Toe raise   b. Calf of leg
_____ Leg curl   c. Quadriceps
_____ Parallel dip   d. Biceps
_____ Arm curls   e. Back of arms
_____ Triceps extension   f. Pectorals

_____ Appendix D: Chapter Evaluations _____

Name _____   Date _____

Chapter 10: The Nautilus Concept

1. According to Nautilus experts, the three primary requirements for muscular growth are:

2. The Nautilus experts believe that _____ repetitions are much more productive than _____ repetitions for strength building.

3. List 6 of the 12 rules for Nautilus training.

4. Nautilus believes that muscle failure should occur between _____ and _____ seconds.

_____ Appendix D: Chapter Evaluations _____ __

TRUE or FALSE

____ 1. A muscle will regain approximately 70% of its initial strength within 30 seconds after fatigue has set in.
____ 2. Anabolic steroids can enhance male potency.
____ 3. Warming up causes an increase in body heat of muscle tissue thus allowing the muscle to contract and relax better.
____ 4. Strength can be maintained by exercising at least once weekly.
____ 5. Stretching exercises should be distributed rather than massed.
____ 6. Ballistic stretching is considered less dangerous than static stretching.
____ 7. Dehydration tends to cause a decrease in blood volume.
____ 8. It is generally recognized that strength in women is about 75% that of men.
____ 9. Bar bell collars should not be used if you are alone and bench pressing free weights.
____ 10. Exercise smaller muscles first then work up to the larger groups.
____ 11. Whenever a muscle fiber contracts, it contracts maximally.
____ 12. Females do not normally acquire the same level of work capacity as males at any age.
____ 13. The average woman has a smaller percentage of muscle in relation to adipose tissue.
____ 14. Hypertrophy is the wasting away of muscle tissue by inactivity.
____ 15. Overload is when exercise is decreased in intensity so that the body can meet the demands.
____ 16. One of the less important factors in determining potential size of a muscle is its length.
____ 17. Holding one's breath while lifting has a tendency to elevate blood pressure and increase body temperature.
____ 18. Research indicates that body conditioning acquired after a four week training program will remain fo four weeks if training is discontinued completely.
____ 19. Isokinetic exercise is the static contraction of a muscle group in which the joint angle and muscle length remain constant.
____ 20. Hypertrophy is the enlargement of muscle tissue.
____ 21. When moving the bar from the floor to the chest it should be kept as close to the body as possible.

_____Appendix E: Weight Training Examination_____

___ 22. Empirical evidence reveals that trainees might profit more by counting time rather than by counting repetitions.
___ 23. Fast repetitions are more productive than slow repetitions for strength building purposes.
___ 24. It is believed that the person with more fast twitch fibers has an advantage in endurance type activities.
___ 25. The human body has approximately 400 muscles.
___ 26. Heart muscle is more efficient than other bodily muscles.
___ 27. "Sticking point" is the term used to describe when the joint angle is most efficient in terms of mechanical efficiency.
___ 28. Muscular endurance is best developed by decreasing the weight and increasing the repetitions.
___ 29. Sloe repetitions are much more productive than fast repetitions for strength building purposes.
___ 30. Just as the resting heart rate slows during sleep, so does the process of restoring body cells.
___ 31. The "flying exercise" is particularly good for developing the pectorals.
___ 32. Endurance exercises increase the production of red blood cells.
___ 33. A static contraction occurs when the muscles which are antagonistic to each other contract with equal strength.
___ 34. It is believed that the ratio of fast twitch and slow twitch muscle fibers can be developed through athletic training.
___ 35. Striated muscles are the skeletal muscles.
___ 36. Stretching should always be slow and deliberate.
___ 37. The use of anabolic steroids has caused cancer in some weight trainers.
___ 38. Individuals vary in the number of fast-twitch and slow-twitch muscle fibers in their muscle tissue.
___ 39. Stretch reflex is the automatic lengthening of a muscle in response to the muscles being suddenly stretched beyond its normal length.
___ 40. There are three variables in exercise: duration, intensity, and frequency. Of three, frequency is the most important in building muscles.
___ 41. One of the most important factors in determining potential size of a muscle is its length.
___ 42. Holding ones breath while lifting has a tendency to elevate blood pressure and increase body temperature.
___ 43. Some researchers contend it is possible for an untrained male to increase his strength 500%.

_____Appendix E: Weight Training Examination_____

___ 44. The pullover or pull down machine is particularly good for developing the latissimus dorsi muscles.
___ 45. A lifter should grip the bar or machine hand grip as tightly as possible to prevent slippage.
___ 46. Weight Training has been used by a number of movie stars for figure trimming.
___ 47. It is highly recommended that during the first 4-6 workouts a person use a heavier than normal load.
___ 48. Muscle measurements should not be taken immediately after a training session.
___ 49. Sit ups with straight legs are generally considered harmful.
___ 50. Arthur Jones spearheaded the nautilus concept.
___ 51. The rowing machine is not particularly effective for the deltoids and trapezius muscles.
___ 52. A motor unit is a group of muscle fibers.
___ 53. Dripping exercises such as push-ups are very effective for the triceps.
___ 54. The quadriceps are located in the upper body.
___ 55. The hamstrings are one of the most powerful muscles in the upper body.

MULTIPLE CHOICE

___ 1. To develop bulk and strength it is best to do low repetitions with high weight for:
a. 12-20 reps   b. 6-12 reps   c. 1-5 reps
d. 20 or more reps

___ 2. For developing muscle endurance it is best to do high reps with low weight for:
a. 6-12 reps   b. 1-5 reps.   c. 12-20 reps

___ 3. Women average out at about 25% of body weight in fat tissue, and men average out at about ___ % in fat tissue.
a. 10   b. 15   c. 20   d. 25   e. 30

___ 4. The absorption of oxygen from the blood into the muscle cells is made possible by:
a. Hemoglobin   b. Myoglobin   c. Striated muscle
d. eccentric contractions   e. concentric contractions

___ 5. The most important principle in building muscles is:
a. intensity   b. frequency   c. duration
d. stretch reflex principle   e. all or nothing principle

_____Appendix E: Weight Training Examination___ __

___ 6. Leg extensions primarily work the _____ muscles.
   a. hamstring   b. quadriceps   c. pectoral
   d. soleus   d. gastrocnemius

___ 7. The shoulder shrug place primary emphasis on the _____ muscles.
   a. biceps   b. triceps   c. abductor
   d. trapezius   e. quadriceps

___ 8. This person was an American army doctor who pioneered the use of weights for physical rehabilitation.
   a. T.L. DeVries   b. L.T. DeLoach   c. T.L. DeLorme
   d. T.R. Tuten   e. Jack Benny

___ 9. A complete lifting workout can efficiently be accomplished in:
   a. 10-20 min.   b. 20-30 min.   c. 30-40 min.
   d. 40-50 min.   e. 50-60 min.

___10. A muscle will be able to perform with 80-90% normal strength within _____ minutes after fatigue has developed.
   a. 3   b. 7 1/2   c. 10 1/2
   d. 13   e. 15

___ 11. As a general rule each repetition should take approximately _____ seconds to perform.
   a. 4   b. 6   c. 8   d. 3   e. 10

___12. A muscle will regain approximately _____% of its initial strength within thirty seconds after fatigue has set in.
   a. 10   b. 30   c. 50   d. 70   e. 90

___13. Leg presses, leg curls and squats primarily develop the:
   a. quadriceps   b. pectorals   c. hamstrings
   d. obliques   e. trapezius

_____Appendix E: Weight Training Examination_____

NAME _____

Exercises:										
	Wt.	1 Reps	Wt.	2 Reps	Wt.	3 Reps	Wt.	4 Reps	Wt.	5 Reps

Appendix F: Blank Charts

NAME _____

Exercises:

Wt. **1** Reps.	Wt. **2** Reps.	Wt. **3** Reps.	Wt. **4** Reps.	Wt. **5** Reps.

Appendix F: Blank Charts

NAME _____

Exercises:	Wt. 1 Reps	Wt. 2 Reps	Wt. 3 Reps	Wt. 4 Reps	Wt. 5 Reps

Appendix F: Blank Charts

NAME _____

Exercises:					
	Wt. 1 Reps.	Wt. 2 Reps.	Wt. 3 Reps.	Wt. 4 Reps.	Wt. 5 Reps.

Appendix F: Blank Charts

NAME _____

Exercises:					
	Wt. 1 Reps	Wt. 2 Reps	Wt. 3 Reps	Wt. 4 Reps	Wt. 5 Reps

Appendix F: Blank Charts

NAME _____

Exercises:					
	Wt 1 Reps	Wt 2 Reps	Wt 3 Reps	Wt 4 Reps	Wt 5 Reps

Appendix F: Blank Charts

NAME _____

Exercises:					
	Wt. 1 Reps.	Wt. 2 Reps.	Wt. 3 Reps.	Wt. 4 Reps.	Wt. 5 Reps.

Appendix F: Blank Charts

NAME _____

Exercises:					
	Wt. 1 Reps	Wt. 2 Reps	Wt. 3 Reps	Wt. 4 Reps	Wt. 5 Reps

Appendix F: Blank Charts

NAME _____

Exercises:					
	Wt. 1 Reps	Wt. 2 Reps	Wt. 3 Reps	Wt. 4 Reps	Wt. 5 Reps

Appendix F: Blank Charts

NAME _____

Exercises:					
	Wt. 1 Reps	Wt. 2 Reps	Wt. 3 Reps	Wt. 4 Reps	Wt. 5 Reps

Appendix F: Blank Charts

INDEX

Abduction, 6
Adduction, 6
Anabolic steroids (see Steroids)
Arm, chest, and shoulder machines, 17-18
    Cybex eagle fly machine, 17
    Schwinn bowflex, 18
    Universal double triceps machine, 17
Athletic benefits, 4

Back pain, 22
Bar, 6, 10
    E-Z curl, 13
Barbells, 11
Bench press, 6
Blitz, 37
Body builders, 4, 41
Body fat, 26-27
Body measurements, 41-43
Box jump, 19
Burn, 36

Circuit training, 38-39
Clean and jerk, 6
Collars, 6
Cooling down, 40
Cooper, Kenneth, 23, 40
Cuts, 6

Dead lift, 6
Dumbbell, 3, 6, 11

Elastic rebound, 6
Endurance exercise, 50
Equipment, 10-19, 82-83
Extension, 6

Fitness benefits, 21-24
Fitnessgram, 23
Flexibility, 54-56
    Exercises, 57-71

Flexion, 6
Fluid replacement, 35-36
Free weight lifts, 85-111
    Abdominals, 87-88
    Arms, 103-106
    Arms-chest, 93-96
    Arms and shoulders, 100-102
    Back, shoulders, arms, 97-99
    Forearm, wrist, fingers, 109-110
    Hips and waist, 85-86
    Legs, 89-92
    Lower back, 102-103
    Neck, 111
    Thighs and hips, 86-87
    Upper arm, 107-108
Fundamentals, 73-79

Harmful exercises, 34
Head strap, 7
High intensity exercise, 40-41
History of weight training, 1-3
Hypertrophy, 7

Incline bench, 12
Incline-decline boards, 7
Iron boots, 7
Isokinetic, 7
Isometric exercise, 7, 38
Isotonic, 7

Lat machine, 7, 16
    Nautilus torso arm machine, 16
    Universal pull down machine, 16
Leg machines, 14-15
    AMF leg press, 15
    Cybex leg press, 15
    Keiser leg extension, 15
    Nautilus leg press, 15
    Universal leg curl, 14
Load, 7

Medical benefits, 4
Motor unit, 47-48
Muscles,
    Contraction, 49-50
        Concentric, 49
        Eccentric, 49
        Static, 49
    Fiber, 46-47
    Function, 24
    Groups, 38, 82-83
    Growth, 25
    Illustration, 210-211
    Number, 24
    Size, 41
    Structure, 45-46
    Types, 48-49
        Cardiac, 48
        Smooth, 48
        Striated, 48
Muscle Bound, 33-34
Muscular endurance, 7

Nautilus concept, 121-151
Negative exercise, 7
Negative accentuated exercise, 8
Negative emphasized exercised, 8
Negative only exercise, 8
Nutrition, 28-29

Olympic lifting, 3,4, 8
Osteoporosis, 23
Overloading, 8, 80

Power, 8
Power clean, 8
Power lifting, 4, 8
Preexhaustion principle, 37

Resistance, 80-81
Reps (repetitions), 8

Set, 80
Scientific principles, 45-50
Smoking, 36
Snatch, 8
Special programs, 153-208
Squat lift, 8
Squat rack, 13
Standards, 8
Steroids, 6, 33
Sticking point, 8
Strength
    Training, 30
    Regaining, 30
        Males vs. Females, 30-33
Stretching, 51-55
    Exercises, 57-71
Superset, 36-37

Turner Society, 3

Universal machine lifts, 113-120
    Chest, back, arms, 115-120
    Legs, 113-115

Warming up, 51
Weights, 10-11
    Nonadjustable, 11
    Interchangeable, 11
Weight control, 26-27
Weight lifters, 4
Wrist straps, 40